hamlyn | all colour cookbook

200 more one pot meals

Joanna Farrow

An Hachette UK Company
www.hachette.co.uk

First published in Great Britain in 2013 by Hamlyn,
a division of Octopus Publishing Group Ltd,
Endeavour House, 189 Shaftesbury Avenue
London, WC2H 8JY
www.octopusbooks.co.uk

ISBN: 978-0-600-62527-8

A CIP catalogue record for this book is available from the
British Library

Printed and bound in China

1 2 3 4 5 6 7 8 9 10

Both metric and imperial measurements have been given
in all recipes. Use one set of measurements only, and not a
mixture of both.

Standard level spoon measurements are used in all recipes.
1 tablespoon = 15 ml spoon
1 teaspoon = 5 ml spoon

Ovens should be preheated to the specified temperature –
if using a fan-assisted oven, follow the manufacturer's
instructions for adjusting the time and temperature.

Fresh herbs should be used unless otherwise stated.
Medium eggs should be used unless otherwise stated.
Freshly ground black pepper should be used unless
otherwise stated.

This book includes dishes made with nuts and nut
derivatives. It is advisable for people with known allergic
reactions to nuts and nut derivatives or those who may be
potentially vulnerable to these allergies, such as pregnant
and nursing mothers, invalids, the elderly, babies and
children, to avoid dishes made with these. It is prudent to
check the labels of all pre-prepared ingredients for the
possible inclusion of nut derivatives.

200 **more** one pot meals

contents

introduction

introduction

When it comes to easy, fuss-free food, you can't do better than cooking one pot meals. These include a feast of delicious dishes, from warming, wintry casseroles and stews to lighter soups, risottos and veggie bakes. As the term implies, the whole dish is cooked in one pot, usually starting with frying off meat, vegetables or fish, then adding various other ingredients and cooking the dish slowly and gently to let the flavours mingle and develop. Not only is the preparation easy but there's little washing up involved and cooking times are flexible too – most one pot dishes won't spoil if left in the oven for longer than you had planned.

equipment

Invest in sturdy, durable utensils for one pot cooking and they will contribute to your one pot successes. Here are a few items you might want to consider buying if you haven't already got them.

flameproof casseroles

These are the most useful of all the one pot utensils, and they feature in many of the recipes in this book. Preparation usually starts on the hob with techniques such as frying off vegetables and meat, before adding other ingredients and transferring the pot to the oven. Flameproof casserole dishes with ovenproof handles are available in various sizes and most are stylish enough to take from oven or hob to table. If you don't have any pans that can be used both on the hob and in the oven, first use a frying pan on the hob and then tip the fried ingredients into an ovenproof casserole dish to finish cooking in the oven.

saucepans

A good-quality, heavy-based saucepan is a good investment and won't buckle, burn or catch during cooking. Its efficient heat conduction means that you can leave the pan on the back burner without the risk of ingredients catching and burning on the base. A sturdy, heavy-based saucepan with double ovenproof handles for easy grip makes a good substitute if you don't have a flameproof casserole.

sauté pans

These wide, shallow pans are deeper than frying pans and useful for recipes where you are gently frying meat or fish before adding stock, wine or other liquids. A large, deep-sided frying pan makes a good substitute because the contents can be stirred without slopping over the sides of the pan.

frying pans

Several of the recipes in this book are cooked in a large heavy-based frying pan that enables you to fry off ingredients successfully and incorporate plenty of other ingredients. Some have lids, but you can use foil, secured around the rim of the pan, or a baking sheet instead.

woks

These are great for simmering, steaming and deep-frying as well as stir-frying. Their rounded base is designed to encourage the heat to encircle the whole pan and cook quickly and evenly. They are also great for recipes where your regular frying pan is not quite large enough to incorporate all the ingredients. Choose a completely round-based wok for a gas hob or one with a slightly flattened base for an electric hob.

baking dishes

Where a one pot recipe is assembled in a dish without the need to fry off any ingredients first, a shallow baking dish that can be taken directly to the table is very useful.

roasting tins

These tins have to endure temperatures that are very high, both in the oven and on the hob, so a good-quality one that doesn't buckle or burn is essential. Some of the recipes require a large tin so that the ingredients have space to roast and colour. Opt for the largest size available that will comfortably fit in your oven.

immersion blenders

Also known as stick or hand-held blenders, these are great for blending soups in the pan you have cooked them in, saving time and effort in washing up. A food processor or blender can be used instead.

9

elements of successful one pot cooking. The process both develops a good flavour and adds a rich colour to stews, casseroles and pot roasts. Make sure the meat is thoroughly dry first, if necessary pressing it between several sheets of kitchen paper, then season and/ or flour the pieces (see below). Heat the fat in the flameproof casserole or frying pan and add some of the meat, spreading the pieces so that each has space around it. Don't add too many pieces at once, otherwise the meat will steam in its own juices. Fry the pieces, shaking the pan gently but do not turn them, until deep brown on the underside. Using a wooden spatula, turn the pieces until browned all over, then drain with a slotted spoon while you fry the next batch. Whole pieces of meat or poultry can also be seared in a pan before pot roasting, using the same process, turning the joint in the fat, and searing the ends. Butter is often combined with oil for frying off (use lightly salted butter). The butter ensures flavour; the oil prevents it burning.

techniques

There are certain simple techniques that are used repeatedly in one pot cooking that you may not be familiar with. The following are worth knowing to produce successful results.

frying off meat

Thoroughly frying off ingredients, particularly meat and poultry, is one of the most crucial

flouring meat

Sometimes meat is floured before frying. This adds colour but is ultimately used to thicken the juices of a stew or casserole as it cooks. Season the flour (as stated in the recipe) with salt and pepper on a plate and turn the prepared meat in the flour with your fingers until coated. Don't discard any excess flour left on the plate – tip it into the pan when frying and it will contribute to thicken the juices.

10

skinning tomatoes

Tomato skins don't soften, even when cooked for some time, so are worth removing. Pull away the stalks, make a slit with a knife and place the tomatoes in a heatproof bowl. Cover with boiling water and leave to stand for about 30 seconds if the tomatoes are very ripe, or a couple of minutes if very firm. Drain and fill the bowl with cold water. Peel away the skins and halve or chop the tomatoes as required.

crushing spices

A small coffee or spice grinder is ideal for crushing spices in seconds. A pestle and mortar is a more traditional method of crushing spices, or you can use a small bowl and the end of a rolling pin. Lay a tea towel over the spices to stop the seeds bouncing out. Don't spend time crushing seeds to a powder – a light pounding is enough.

jointing a chicken or guinea fowl

A few of the recipes in this book require a jointed chicken or guinea fowl, which may not be available to buy. Follow these simple steps to jointing your own. It's a useful skill to have and the bones can be kept to make stock (see page 36).

1 Cut vertically down through the skin and flesh between the leg and breast on one side of the bird. Pull the leg away from the body until the ball and socket joint at the carcass end of the thigh is exposed. Bend the leg back so that the joint snaps apart, then use the tip of the knife to release the meat around the joint. Remove the leg on the other side in the same way.

2 To make the wing portions meatier, a small piece of breast meat can be removed with them. Hold the wing and make a diagonal cut down through the back of the breast.

3 Feel around for the wing joint with the knife to locate the socket. Cut through this and remove completely. Repeat on the other side.

4 Cut vertically down one side of the breastbone. Keeping the knife against the rib cage to avoid wasting any meat, pull the breast meat back with one hand as you ease the flesh away from the ribs with a knife. Repeat on the other side.

5 Place a leg joint, skin-side down, on the board. Bend the leg so that you can see where the joint is located. (There is usually a thin piece of white fat over the joint where you need to aim the knife.) Cut down through this to divide the leg into 2 pieces. Repeat with the other leg.

6 Cut each breast portion across into 2 pieces.

ingredients

Choose good-quality ingredients and you are halfway to making the perfect one pot meal. Keep your storecupboard stocked with a supply of rice, lentils, oils, spices, flavourings and condiments, and buy the best fresh ingredients you can.

meat

Beef should be a deep dark red, sometimes almost purple, with a marbling of fat running through the lean meat. These thread-like traces of white fat help keep the meat moist and succulent as it cooks. The surface fat should be creamy coloured, and both fat and

lean should look dry, not wet. Look for 'dry-aged' beef that will have been aged naturally. Lamb should also be very red, though the colour will depend more on the age of the lamb. Pork fat should look whiter and the flesh rosy pink, again with no wateriness. Chops and steaks should be of similar thickness so that they cook evenly. Bone ends should be neatly sawn, not splintered, and rolled joints should be professionally and neatly tied. Avoid buying cuts from which all the fat has been trimmed off, as it's the fat that provides so much flavour and succulence while the meat cooks.

fish
Choose whole fish with bright, plump eyes rather than sunken dried ones. The fish should have a glossy, fresh sheen and plumpness as though they have only just been caught. The bodies should be firm with bellies intact rather than split (which might be an indication of staleness), particularly when it comes to oily fish. Fillets should look moist and succulent with flesh that holds together firmly. Avoid dull, ragged, dry-looking pieces. Oily fish like mackerel, sardines and herrings deteriorate quickly, so be particularly careful when choosing these.

Essential herbs

Basil Highly fragrant and aromatic, delicate basil leaves are best removed from their stems and roughly chopped or torn into dishes towards the end of cooking. Used mainly in Mediterranean dishes, particularly tomato based ones.

Bay These hardy leaves are added to one pot dishes at the beginning of cooking because the flavour takes a while to emerge. Bay combines well with parsley and thyme and is mostly used in slow cooked meaty dishes.

Chives Has a mild onion flavour and very useful for adding a fresh burst of flavour to summery stews and casseroles as well as salad accompaniments. Finely chop or snip the leaves with scissors. Particularly good in fish, chicken and vegetable dishes.

Coriander Easily confused with flat leaf parsley, coriander has more rounded, delicate leaves. Chop both the leaves and stalks into spicy dishes. Use plenty for sprinking on top too as its aroma really stimulates the appetite.

Dill Delicate, feathery leaves resemble fennel tops (which make a good substitute) with a mild aniseed flavour. Discard any thick stalks and finely chop the rest into fish and vegetable dishes.

Oregano Hardy oregano leaves are best removed from their stalks and finely chopped into meat, chicken or veggie one pot dishes. Widely used in those with a Greek or Italian flavour, dried oregano is a commonly used substitute.

Parsley Both 'curly' and 'flat leaf' varieties are indispensible in meat, fish and veggie one pot dishes. Stalks and leaves are used.

Rosemary Pull the needle-like leaves from the stems and finely chop for adding to dishes, or use the whole sprigs. Use chopped rosemary quite sparingly. Particularly good with lamb dishes.

Sage Green, variegated and purple varieties are all used, either chopped or whole. Sage is good with meat and veggie dishes, in particular pork and bacon.

Tarragon Delicate, spindle tarragon leaves have a mild aniseed flavour and should be pulled from their stalks and chopped into chicken, pork, fish and veggie dishes.

Thyme The many varieties of thyme are all useful in almost all slow cooked one pot dishes. The tiny leaves of hardy thyme should be pulled from their stalks and added at the beginning of cooking while the tender, young stalks can be chopped and added later on.

herbs: fresh & frozen

Herbs are one of the most appetizing ingredients to add to any dish and can be used liberally, their fragrant, aromatic flavours mingling with and complementing almost any meat, fish or veggie dish. Hardier herbs like bay, thyme and rosemary are usually added to a dish early on in the cooking process, whereas more delicate herbs are stirred in at the end. Frozen herbs are a useful standby, particularly delicate ones like chives, tarragon, fennel and dill. If you have bought too many fresh ones or have a glut, chop them and freeze in bags for later use.

oils

Most of the recipes use olive oil for frying, which is particularly appropriate for Mediterranean dishes. Some olive oils are infused with flavours like basil, garlic and chilli. These are also good for frying, though chilli oil is best used sparingly, as some brands are very hot. Other recipes require a vegetable oil such as sunflower, corn or groundnut oil. A couple of Asian dishes use stir-fry or wok oil. These are seasoned with flavours such as garlic and ginger, though you can use an ordinary vegetable oil instead.

flavoured oils

These are easy to make yourself and are worth doing when you've got herbs left from a recipe or plentiful supplies in the garden. Use a single herb or combine several in one oil. Use a light olive oil or sunflower oil as the base. Pack herbs such as rosemary, basil, thyme, bay, oregano or tarragon into a bottle. Several cloves of garlic or pared strips of lemon can also be added. Fill the bottles with oil. Leave to stand in a cool place for several weeks, shaking frequently. Strain the oil into a clean bottle, adding fresh herb sprigs for presentation (This also looks good if making as a present). Store in a cool place. For homemade chilli oil, see page 216.

garlic

If you're not a fan of garlic it can be left out of a one pot recipe. If you love it, then be really

generous. Garlic keeps well in the fridge but will gradually stale so check before use: it should be firm and juicy, not dry and greying. Garlic presses are good for crushing but using a board and sharp knife is quick and easy and saves on washing up. To crush by hand, press the side of a large knife firmly down on a clove with the heel of your hand. This detaches the skin and softens the flesh. Peel away the skin and chop the clove to break it up. Continue to crush the garlic by mashing it onto the board with the side of the knife. A little salt sprinkled over the garlic as you work will help break it down and stop the knife sliding around.

fresh root ginger

Hot and fragrant, fresh root ginger is a staple addition to one pot meals, particularly Asian and Indian dishes. Choose plump roots that are not too knobbly for easy peeling. Cut away knobbly areas that are difficult to peel then use a potato peeler or scrape the ginger with the edge of a teaspoon to remove the skin. Finely chop or grate, catch and use the juices.

saffron

Expensive but exotic, saffron is useful in fish and spiced dishes, including a classic paella. It can be crumbled directly into the pan or steeped in boiling water first to release its flavour. Crumble with your fingers into a small heatproof bowl. Add a tablespoon of boiling water and leave to infuse for several minutes. Use both strands and liquid.

wine

Both red and white wine make delicious additions to one pot dishes from hearty meat and game dishes to lighter fish or veggie ones. As a general rule, use an inexpensive wine (but one you'd drink). In most cases it's red for meat and game and white for chicken and fish. If you've got some leftover wine that needs using up, add it to a 'one pot' in place of an equal measure of stock.

spices

A good supply of spices adds plenty of variety to one pot cooking but will deteriorate over time. Check any you have had in store for a while – if they have lost their spicy aroma, or simply have no aroma at all, throw them away. For most recipes it's best to buy whole seeds such as cumin, coriander, fennel and cardamom and grind them yourself (see page 11).

stock

A flavour-packed stock is essential to so many one pot dishes, whether fish, meat, poultry or vegetable. There are now some good-quality powdered stocks that make great storecupboard standbys, as well as liquid concentrates and shop-bought ready-made stocks. Some of these are vacuum packed and don't need refrigeration, while those from the chiller cabinet will last several days. The best option is to make your own when fresh or cooked bones are available. It takes just a few minutes to get the stock pot going, and the rest takes care of itself. Once made, all cooled, strained stocks can be frozen in airtight containers or freezer bags for up to six months. See the individual recipes for homemade stock: chicken, page 36; beef, page 108; lamb, page 110; vegetable, page 210.

tomato purée

A storecupboard essential, tomato purée is an intense tomato concentrate that adds concentrated flavour and colour to many one pot dishes. Sun-dried tomato paste has a sweeter flavour and is perfect for Mediterranean dishes.

accompaniments

The recipes in this book are designed to be complete dishes. But to satisfy hungry appetites, a well-flavoured bread warmed through before the dish is ready is the most effortless accompaniment to one pot dining and makes a delicious vehicle for mopping up the tasty juices. Alternatively a dish of creamy mashed potato or buttery greens make great partners to a wintry stew. A mixed or leafy herb salad is an easy accompaniment. Ready-cooked rice and noodles make useful standbys, too, and are easy to reheat. Stir into a dish before serving. Couscous and bulgar wheat make fuss-free accompaniments, particularly for North African and Middle Eastern dishes.

poultry & game

chicken mole

Serves **4**
Preparation time **25 minutes**
Cooking time **1½ hours**

3 tablespoons **vegetable oil**
1 **chicken**, about 1.5 kg (3 lb),
   jointed (see page 12)
1 **onion**, chopped
1 **green pepper**, cored,
   deseeded and chopped
½ teaspoon **ground allspice**
½ teaspoon **ground
   cinnamon**
½ teaspoon **ground cumin**
1 teaspoon **chilli powder**
2 **garlic cloves**, crushed
200 g (7 oz) **can chopped
   tomatoes**
300 ml (½ pint) **chicken stock**
   (see page 38 for homemade)
25 g (1 oz) bought or homemade corn **tortilla**
40 g (1½ oz) **blanched
   almonds**, roughly chopped
2 tablespoons **sesame seeds**,
   plus extra for sprinkling
15 g (½ oz) **plain dark
   chocolate** (85% cocoa
   solids), roughly chopped
salt and **pepper**
chopped **fresh coriander**,
   to garnish

Heat the oil in a flameproof casserole and fry the chicken pieces for 5 minutes until golden on all sides. Drain to a plate. Add the onion and green pepper to the casserole and fry gently for 5 minutes until softened, stirring in the spices and garlic for the last few minutes.

Add the tomatoes and half the stock and bring to the boil. Return the chicken to the pan, cover and cook in a hot oven, 180°C (350°F), Gas Mark 4, for 45 minutes.

Meanwhile, tear the tortilla into pieces and place in a food processor with the almonds and sesame seeds. Process until finely ground. Pour in the remaining stock and process again until smooth. Stir the almond mixture and chocolate into the casserole and return to the oven for a further 30 minutes until the chicken is cooked through and tender.

Season to taste with salt and pepper, then sprinkle with extra sesame seeds and scatter with chopped coriander to garnish. Serve with warmed tortillas, if liked.

For homemade corn tortillas, mix together 225 g (7½ oz) masa harina flour and ½ teaspoon salt in a bowl. Add 1 tablespoon lemon juice and 225 ml (7½ fl oz) tepid water and mix to a dough, adding a dash more water if the dough feels dry. Knead into a smooth dough and leave to stand, covered with clingfilm, for 30 minutes. Divide the dough into 8 pieces and shape into balls. Roll each ball out flat on a lightly floured surface. Heat a dry frying pan or griddle and cook for about 1 minute on each side or until beginning to colour. Serve, or wrap in foil and reheat in a preheated oven, 180°C (350°F), Gas Mark 4, for 15 minutes, then serve.

pot-roast pheasant with croutons

Serves **5–6**
Preparation time **10 minutes**,
  plus soaking
Cooking time **2 hours**

20 g (¾ oz) **mixed dried
  mushrooms**
300 ml (½ pint) **boiling water**
2 **pheasants**
40 g (1½ oz) **butter**
2 tablespoons **vegetable oil**
100 g (3½ oz) **smoked
  streaky bacon**, chopped
2 **small onions**, chopped
2 **small parsnips**, diced
2 **garlic cloves**, crushed,
  plus 1 **plump garlic
  clove**, peeled
1 tablespoon **plain flour**
300 ml (½ pint) **red wine**
1 tablespoon **chopped thyme**
1 small **baguette**
2 tablespoons **redcurrant jelly**
salt and **pepper**

Place the dried mushrooms in a heatproof bowl and pour over the water. Leave to soak for 10 minutes.

Rinse the pheasants and pat dry with kitchen paper. Season with salt and pepper.

Melt the butter with the oil in a large flameproof casserole and fry the pheasants, one at a time, for 5 minutes until golden on all sides, draining to a plate. Add the bacon, onions, parsnips and garlic to the casserole and fry for 5 minutes. Sprinkle in the flour and cook, stirring, for 1 minute. Remove from the heat and blend in the wine, then stir in the mushrooms and their soaking liquid and the thyme. Bring to a simmer, stirring.

Return the pheasants to the casserole, nestling them into the vegetables. Cover and cook in a preheated oven, 150°C (300°F), Gas Mark 2, for 1¾ hours or until the pheasants are cooked through. Meanwhile, cut the baguette into thin slices and toast on both sides. Halve the garlic clove and rub the cut sides over the toast.

Transfer the pheasants to a board or carving platter, cover with foil and keep warm. Add the redcurrant jelly to the casserole and stir until melted. Season to taste with salt and pepper. Carve the pheasants and pile the meat on to the croutons on warmed serving plates. Spoon over the vegetables and gravy.

For chicken & black pudding pot roast, make the recipe as above using a 1.75 kg (3½ lb) chicken instead of the pheasants and omitting the parsnips. Skin and chop 200 g (7 oz) black pudding and add to the casserole with the mushrooms and thyme. Replace the redcurrant jelly with 2 tablespoons bramble jelly.

lemon chilli chicken

Serves **4**
Preparation time **25 minutes**,
plus marinating
Cooking time **45 minutes**

1 **chicken**, about 1.75 kg
(3½ lb), jointed (see
page 12)
8 **garlic cloves**, peeled
4 **juicy lemons**, quartered and
squeezed, skins reserved
1 **small red chilli**, deseeded
and chopped
2 tablespoons **orange
blossom honey**
4 tablespoons **chopped
parsley**, plus sprigs
to garnish
salt and **pepper**

Arrange the chicken pieces in a shallow flameproof dish. Crush 2 of the garlic cloves and add them to the lemon juice with the chilli and honey. Stir well, then pour the mixture over the chicken. Tuck the lemon skins around the meat, cover and leave to marinate in the refrigerator for at least 2 hours or overnight, turning once or twice.

Turn the chicken pieces skin-side up, scatter over the remaining whole garlic cloves and place the lemon skins, cut-side down, on top.

Cook the chicken in a preheated oven, 200°C (400°F), Gas Mark 6, for 45 minutes or until golden brown, cooked through and tender. Stir in the chopped parsley, season to taste with salt and pepper and serve garnished with parsley sprigs.

For coriander rice & peas, to serve as an accompaniment, bring a large saucepan of lightly salted water to the boil and add 250 g (8 oz) white long-grain rice, then reduce the heat and simmer for about 15 minutes until tender. Drain well. Meanwhile, cook 250 g (8 oz) frozen peas in a separate saucepan of lightly salted boiling water for about 3 minutes. Drain and toss with 50 g (2 oz) melted butter, 2 chopped spring onions and a handful of chopped fresh coriander. Fork the pea mixture into the cooked rice.

rabbit & mushroom risotto

Serves **4**
Preparation time **25 minutes**
Cooking time **40 minutes**

65 g (2½ oz) **butter**
150 g (5 oz) **chestnut mushrooms**, trimmed and sliced
250 g (8 oz) **boneless lean rabbit**, diced
1 **onion**, chopped
1 **celery stick**, diced
3 **garlic cloves**, crushed
1 teaspoon finely **chopped thyme**
300 g (10 oz) **risotto rice**
300 ml (½ pint) **red wine**
800 ml (1 pint 7fl oz) **hot chicken stock** (see page 36 for homemade)
4 tablespoons **chopped parsley**
salt and **pepper**

Melt 15 g (½ oz) of the butter in a large saucepan and fry the mushrooms for about 5 minutes until lightly browned. Lift out with a slotted spoon on to a plate and set aside.

Season the rabbit lightly with salt and pepper. Melt another 25 g (1 oz) of the butter in the pan and fry the rabbit for 5 minutes, until beginning to colour. Add the onion and celery and fry gently, stirring frequently, for about 5 minutes until the vegetables have softened.

Stir in the garlic, thyme and rice and cook, stirring, for 1 minute. Add the wine and cook quickly until the wine has been absorbed. Gradually add the hot stock to the pan, a ladleful at a time, and cook, stirring frequently, until each ladleful has mostly been absorbed before adding the next. This should take 20–25 minutes, by which time the rice should be tender but retaining a little bite and the consistency should be creamy. You may not need all the stock.

Return the mushrooms to the pan and stir in the remaining butter and the parsley. Season to taste with salt and pepper and serve immediately.

For chicken, Stilton & thyme risotto, make the risotto as above, omitting the mushrooms fried in butter and using 250 g (8 oz) diced boneless, skinless chicken instead of the rabbit and 150 ml (¼ pint) white wine in place of the red wine. Once the risotto is cooked, crumble in 100 g (3½ oz) Stilton cheese instead of the remaining butter and stir through until melted.

poussin with walnut & tarragon

Serves **4**
Preparation time **20 minutes**
Cooking time **1½ hours**

4 **poussin**
50 g (2 oz) **butter**
1 tablespoon **olive oil**
75 g (3 oz) **walnuts**, chopped
625 g (1¼ lb) **courgettes**,
   thickly sliced
1 **large onion**, chopped
3 **garlic cloves**, chopped
150 ml (3½ fl oz) **chicken
stock** (see page 36 for
homemade)
5 g (¼ oz) **tarragon leaves**
100 ml (¼ pint) **soured cream**
salt and **pepper**

Rinse the poussin and pat dry with kitchen paper. Season all over with salt and pepper. Melt half the butter with the oil in a large flameproof casserole and fry the walnuts for a couple of minutes until beginning to colour. Lift out with a slotted spoon on to a plate. Add the courgettes to the casserole and fry for about 5 minutes until lightly browned on both sides. Lift out on to the plate and set aside.

Melt the remaining butter in the casserole and fry the onion for 2 minutes. Add the poussin and fry for 5 minutes until golden on all sides. Add the garlic and stock and bring to the boil. Cover with a lid or foil and cook in a preheated oven, 180°C (350°F), Gas Mark 4, for 45 minutes. Add the tarragon leaves to the casserole with the walnuts and courgettes, then return to the oven for a further 30 minutes.

Lift the poussin from the pan on to warmed serving plates. Drain the walnuts and courgettes on to the plates with a slotted spoon. Stir the soured cream into the sauce and bring to the boil. Check the seasoning, then spoon on to the plates. Serve with grainy bread or creamy mash, if liked.

For poussin with tomatoes & pine nuts, replace the walnuts with 50 g (2 oz) pine nuts, and fry in the butter then set aside as above. Omit the courgettes and fry the onion, then fry the poussin and garlic as above. Add a 400 g (13 oz) can chopped tomatoes, 1 teaspoon caster sugar and 3 tablespoons sun-dried tomato paste with the stock. Cook in the oven as above, adding 3 tablespoons chopped oregano and the pine nuts for the final 30 minutes of cooking time.

turkey & ham casserole

Serves **6**
Preparation time **20 minutes**
Cooking time **1 hour 45 minutes**

350 g (12 oz) **cooked ham** in one piece
2 tablespoons **plain flour**
625 g (1¼ lb) **turkey breast meat**
50 g (2 oz) **butter**
2 **onions**, chopped
2 **celery sticks**, sliced
750 ml (1¼ pints) **chicken stock** (see page 36 for homemade)
1 tablespoon **chopped thyme**
½ teaspoon **mild chilli powder**
300 g (10 oz) **sweet potatoes**, scrubbed and cut into small chunks
150 g (5 oz) **cranberries**
100 ml (3½ fl oz) **crème fraîche**
salt and **pepper**

Cut the ham into dice. Season the flour with a little salt and pepper on a plate. Cut the turkey into small chunks and coat with the seasoned flour.

Melt the butter in a flameproof casserole and fry the turkey for 5 minutes until golden on all sides. Add the onions and celery to the casserole and fry for 4–5 minutes until softened. Tip in any remaining flour left on the plate. Blend in the stock, add the thyme and chilli powder and bring to a simmer, stirring.

Cover the casserole and cook in a preheated oven, 180°C (350°F), Gas Mark 4, for 45 minutes.

Stir the sweet potatoes and ham into the casserole and return to the oven for a further 30 minutes. Stir in the cranberries and crème fraîche and season to taste with salt and pepper. Return to the oven for a final 15 minutes before serving.

For turkey, ham & mushroom pie, trim and slice 250 g (8 oz) mushrooms. Make the recipe as above, lifting the turkey and vegetables out with a slotted spoon onto a plate after frying. Fry the mushrooms in another 15 g (½ oz) butter before returning the turkey and vegetables to the casserole. Cook as above, omitting the sweet potatoes but adding the ham. Leave to cool. Roll out 350 g (12 oz) ready-made puff pastry on a lightly floured surface to the same diameter as the casserole dish and rest the pastry over the filling. (If the casserole dish is very big, transfer the filling to a pie dish.) Brush with beaten egg to glaze and bake in a preheated oven, 200°C (400°F), Gas Mark 6, for 40 minutes or until the pastry is deep golden.

slow-roast duck with redcurrants

Serves **4**

Preparation time **25 minutes**

Cooking time **2 hours 15 minutes**

4 large **duck legs**

¾ teaspoon **ground cinnamon**

1 kg (2 lb) **potatoes**, cut into 1.5 cm (¾ inch) dice

300 g (10 oz) **turnips**, cut into thin wedges

8 **garlic cloves**, peeled but left whole

1 tablespoon **roughly chopped thyme**

100 g (3½ oz) **redcurrants**

150 ml (¼ pint) **chicken stock** (see page 36 for homemade)

3 tablespoons **redcurrant jelly**

4 tablespoons **crème fraîche**

salt and **pepper**

Halve the duck legs by cutting each through the joints. Mix the cinnamon with a little salt and pepper and rub over the duck legs. Arrange in a large roasting tin and roast in a preheated oven, 150°C (300°F), Gas Mark 2, for 1¼ hours.

Drain off most of the fat in the roasting tin, leaving just enough to coat the vegetables. Increase the oven temperature to 200°C (400°F), Gas Mark 6.

Add the potatoes, turnips, garlic and thyme to the roasting tin, turning them in the oil and seasoning lightly with salt and pepper. Return the roasting tin to the oven for 45 minutes until the vegetables are deep golden, turning frequently. Meanwhile, string the redcurrants by passing them between the tines of a fork.

Transfer the duck legs and vegetables to warmed serving plates and keep warm. Drain off the excess fat in the roasting tin, leaving the meaty juices. Add the stock, redcurrant jelly and crème fraîche and bring to the boil on the hob. Cook until slightly reduced and thickened. Stir in the redcurrants, season to taste with salt and pepper and heat for 1 minute. Spoon over the duck to serve.

For buttered beans & courgettes, to serve as an accompaniment, steam 200 g (7 oz) topped and tailed French beans for 5 minutes until tender. Add 300 g (10 oz) thickly sliced courgettes and steam for 2 minutes. Turn into a warmed serving dish and add 40 g (1½ oz) butter, 3 tablespoons chopped chives, 2 tablespoons chopped parsley and a little salt and pepper. Stir until the butter has melted and serve hot.

chicken mulligatawny

Serves **6**
Preparation time **20 minutes**
Cooking time **1½ hours**

50 g (2 oz) **butter**
600 g (1 lb 3 oz) **bone-in, skinless chicken thighs**
2 **onions**, chopped
2 **small carrots**, chopped
1 **small cooking apple**, peeled, cored and chopped
1 tablespoon **plain flour**
1 litre (1¾ pints) **chicken stock** (see below for homemade)
2 tablespoons **mild curry paste**
2 tablespoons **tomato purée**
50 g (2 oz) **basmati rice**
natural yogurt, for topping
salt and **pepper**

Melt half the butter in a saucepan and fry the chicken thighs in two batches for 5 minutes each, until golden on all sides. Lift out with a slotted spoon on to a plate. Add the remaining butter and fry the onions, carrots and apple, stirring, for 6–8 minutes until lightly browned.

Sprinkle in the flour and cook, stirring, for 1 minute. Gradually blend in the stock, then stir in the curry paste, tomato purée and rice. Return the chicken to the pan and bring to a simmer, stirring. Reduce the heat, cover and cook very gently for 1 hour until the chicken is cooked through and very tender.

Lift the chicken pieces from the pan. Once cool enough to handle, pull the meat from the bones. Shred half the meat into pieces and return the remainder to the pan. Blend the soup using an immersion blender or in a food processor.

Return the shredded chicken to the pan and heat through. Season to taste with salt and pepper and serve in bowls topped with spoonfuls of natural yogurt.

For homemade chicken stock, place 1 large chicken carcass or 500 g (1 lb) chicken bones in a large saucepan and add 2 halved, unpeeled onions, 2 roughly chopped carrots, 1 roughly chopped celery stick, several bay leaves and 1 teaspoon black or white peppercorns. Just cover with cold water and bring to a gentle simmer. Reduce the heat to its lowest setting and cook, uncovered, for 2 hours. Strain through a fine sieve and leave to cool. Cover and store in the refrigerator for up to several days or freeze for up to 6 months.

venison, stout & chestnut stew

Serves **6**

Preparation time **25 minutes**

Cooking time **2 hours 15 minutes**

3 tablespoons **plain flour**

1.25 kg (2½ lb) **venison**, diced

50 g (2 oz) **butter**

200 g (7 oz) **pancetta** or **streaky bacon**, chopped

1 **small leek**, trimmed, cleaned and chopped

3 **carrots**, diced

2 **parsnips**, diced

4 **garlic cloves**, crushed

2 teaspoons **chopped rosemary**

500 ml (17 fl oz) **stout**

300 ml (½ pint) **beef stock** (see page 108 for homemade)

200 g (7 oz) **pack cooked peeled chestnuts**

500 g (1 lb) **new potatoes**, scrubbed and cut into small chunks

salt and **pepper**

Season the flour with salt and pepper on a plate. Coat the venison with the flour.

Melt the butter in a flameproof casserole and fry the venison in batches until browned, lifting out with a slotted spoon on to a plate. Add the pancetta or bacon, leek, carrots and parsnips to the casserole and fry gently for 6–8 minutes until lightly browned. Add the garlic, rosemary and any flour left over from coating, and cook, stirring, for 1 minute.

Blend in the stout and stock and bring to a simmer, stirring. Return the venison to the casserole, then reduce the heat, cover and cook very gently for 1½ hours or until the meat is tender.

Add the chestnuts and potatoes and cook for a further 20 minutes or until the potatoes are cooked through. Season to taste with salt and pepper.

For pheasant, red wine & shallot stew, place 300 g (10 oz) shallots in a heatproof bowl, cover with boiling water and leave to stand for 2 minutes. Drain and rinse in cold water. Peel away the skins, leaving the shallots whole. Make the recipe as above, using 1.25 kg (2½ lb) diced pheasant instead of the venison and adding the shallots when frying the vegetables. Then replace the stout with 500 ml (17 fl oz) red wine, 2 tablespoons tomato purée and 1 tablespoon dark muscovado sugar, and omit the chestnuts.

chicken with spring vegetables

Serves **4**

Preparation time **10 minutes**, plus resting

Cooking time about **1 ¼ hours**

1 **chicken**, about 1.5 kg (3 lb)

about 1.5 litres (2½ pints) **hot chicken stock** (see page 36 for homemade)

2 **shallots**, halved

2 **garlic cloves**, peeled but left whole

2 **parsley sprigs**

2 **marjoram sprigs**

2 **lemon thyme sprigs**

2 **carrots**, halved

1 **leek**, trimmed, cleaned and sliced

200 g (7 oz) **tenderstem broccoli**

250 g (8 oz) **asparagus spears**, trimmed

½ **Savoy cabbage**, shredded

crusty bread, to serve

Place the chicken in a large saucepan and pour over enough stock just to cover the chicken. Push the shallots, garlic, herbs, carrots and leek into the pan and bring to the boil, then reduce the heat and simmer gently for 1 hour or until the chicken is falling away from the bones.

Add the remaining vegetables to the pan and simmer for a further 6–8 minutes or until the vegetables are cooked.

Turn off the heat and leave to rest for 5–10 minutes before serving the chicken and vegetables in deep bowls with spoonfuls of the broth. (Remove the chicken skin, if preferred.) Accompany with plenty of crusty bread.

For Chinese chicken soup, cook the recipe as above, replacing the shallots, herbs, carrots and leek with a 7 cm (3 inch) piece of fresh root ginger, peeled and thinly sliced, 2 sliced garlic cloves, 1 teaspoon Chinese five-spice powder, 4–5 star anise and 100 ml (3½ fl oz) dark soy sauce. Then add 250 g (8 oz) each baby corn and mangetout to the pan instead of the broccoli, asparagus and cabbage and simmer for a few minutes until just cooked, before serving.

duck with fruited bulgar wheat

Serves **4**
Preparation time **25 minutes**,
  plus marinating
Cooking time **25 minutes**

4 **duck breasts**, about
  150–175 g (5–6 oz) each
2 teaspoons **harissa paste**
2 teaspoons **coriander seeds**,
  crushed
2 **garlic cloves**, crushed
3 tablespoons **olive oil**
200 g (7 oz) **bulgar wheat**
600 ml (1 pint) **chicken stock**
  (see page 36 for homemade)
75 g (3 oz) **hazelnuts**, roughly
  chopped
75 g (3 oz) **ready-to-eat dried
  apricots**, thinly sliced
150 g (5 oz) **mangetout**,
  thinly sliced
2 tablespoons **pomegranate
  molasses**
2 teaspoons **dark muscovado
  sugar**
seeds of 1 **pomegranate**
salt and **pepper**

Use a small sharp knife to score several deep cuts through the skin side of each duck breast and place in a shallow non-metallic dish. Mix together the harissa, coriander and garlic and spread all over the duck breasts. Cover loosely and leave to marinate in the refrigerator for at least 30 minutes, up to several hours.

Scrape the marinade off the duck breasts and reserve. Heat 1 tablespoon of the oil in a large heavy-based frying pan, add the duck breasts, skin-side down, and cook for 3–4 minutes or until the skin is deep golden. Turn, cook for a further 2 minutes. Transfer to a plate.

Add the bulgar wheat, stock and reserved marinade to the pan. Bring to a simmer, then reduce the heat, cover with a lid or foil and cook very gently for 5 minutes until the bulgar wheat is softened. Stir in the hazelnuts and apricots and return the duck to the pan, pushing the breasts down into the bulgar wheat. Cook gently for a further 8–12 minutes (or 15–20 minutes if you prefer the duck well cooked). Scatter the mangetout into the pan once the duck is cooked to your liking.

Stir the pomegranate molasses and sugar into the bulgar wheat, drizzle with the remaining oil and add salt and pepper. Serve sprinkled with pomegranate seeds.

For chicken & bulgar pilaf, replace the duck with 4 chicken breasts cut horizontally in half to make 8 thin fillets. Marinate as above. Roughly chop 75 g (3 oz) pistachio nuts and 75 g (3 oz) dried figs, discarding the hard stalks. Cook the chicken as the duck, above, using the pistachio nuts and figs instead of hazelnuts and apricots, making sure the chicken is cooked through.

halloumi & aubergine chicken

Serves **4**
Preparation time **25 minutes**
Cooking time **50 minutes**

4 **boneless, skinless chicken breasts**, about 125–150 g (4–5 oz) each
100 g (3½ oz) **halloumi cheese**
several **mint sprigs**, chopped
6 tablespoons **olive oil**
1 **onion**, chopped
1 **fennel bulb**, trimmed and finely chopped
750 g (1½ lb) **aubergines**, cut into 1.5 cm (¾ inch) chunks
3 **garlic cloves**, crushed
450 ml (¾ pint) **chicken** or **vegetable stock** (see pages 36 and 208 for homemade)
5 tablespoons **sun-dried tomato paste**
1 teaspoon **dried oregano**
salt and **pepper**

Lay the chicken breasts on a board. To create a large pocket for the stuffing, use a small sharp knife to make a horizontal cut in the centre of each breast without cutting right through to the other side.

Dice the cheese into a bowl and stir in the mint and a little pepper to season. Pack the mixture into the chicken breast pockets and secure in place with wooden cocktail sticks.

Heat 2 tablespoons of the oil in a large heavy-based frying pan and fry the chicken breasts for 5 minutes, until golden on both sides. Transfer to a plate. Add a further 2 tablespoons of the oil to the pan and gently fry the onion, fennel and half the aubergines for 5 minutes, stirring, until lightly browned. Remove from the pan. Fry the remaining aubergines in the last of the oil for 5 minutes, adding the garlic once the aubergines have browned.

Return all the vegetables to the pan and stir in the stock, tomato paste and oregano. Bring to a simmer. Push the chicken breasts down into the aubergines and reduce the heat to its lowest setting. Cook for about 30 minutes, stirring frequently, until the chicken is cooked through and the aubergines are tender. Season to taste with salt and pepper and serve.

For basil & yogurt sauce, to serve as a side dish, tear 15 g (½ oz) basil leaves into small pieces. Mix together 100 ml (3½ fl oz) Greek yogurt and 75 ml (3 fl oz) soured cream in a bowl with 1 crushed garlic clove, a squeeze of lemon juice and the basil. Turn into a serving dish, cover with clingfilm and chill until ready to serve.

guinea fowl & sausage hotpot

Serves **5–6**
Preparation time **20 minutes**
Cooking time **1¾ hours**

1 **guinea fowl**, about 1 kg
(2 lb), jointed (see page 12)
50 g (2 oz) **butter**
1 tablespoon **vegetable oil**
6 **pork sausages**
2 **carrots**, sliced
2 **leeks**, trimmed, cleaned
and sliced
1½ tablespoons **plain flour**
450 ml (¾ pint) **chicken stock**
(see page 36 for homemade)
150 ml (¼ pint) **red wine**
1 teaspoon **juniper berries**,
crushed with pestle
and mortar
1 kg (2 lb) **potatoes**
salt and **pepper**

Season the guinea fowl pieces on all sides. Melt half the butter with the oil in a shallow flameproof casserole and fry the guinea fowl pieces for 5 minutes, until golden on all sides. Drain and reserve. Fry the sausages for 5 minutes, until browned all over. Transfer to a plate.

Add the remaining butter to the casserole and gently fry the carrots and leeks for 5 minutes until softened. Sprinkle in the flour and cook, stirring, for 1 minute. Remove from the heat and blend in the stock and wine. Stir in the juniper berries. Bring to the boil, stirring, then reduce the heat to a gentle simmer. Return the guinea fowl to the pan, cover and cook gently for 30 minutes.

Slice the potatoes thinly and arrange over the casserole. Season to taste. Cover with the lid or foil and cook in a preheated oven, 180°C (350°F), Gas Mark 4, for 30 minutes. Dot the potatoes with the remaining butter and return to the oven, for 30 minutes until the potatoes are crisped and browned. (Pop the casserole under a preheated grill for a few minutes if desired.)

For easy butter pastry, as an alternative to the potato topping, place 250 g (8 oz) plain flour in a bowl and grate in 150 g (5 oz) butter, stirring it into the flour frequently so that it doesn't clump. Add 2 egg yolks and 5 tablespoons cold water and mix with a round-bladed knife to a firm dough, adding a dash more water if the dough feels dry and crumbly. Wrap and chill for 30 minutes. Make the casserole as above, extending the initial cooking time to 50 minutes. Leave to cool, then cover with the rolled-out pastry. Brush with beaten egg and bake in a preheated oven, 200°C (400°F), Gas Mark 6, for 40 minutes until the pastry is golden.

chicken & sweet potato wedges

Serves **4**
Preparation time **20 minutes**
Cooking time **35 minutes**

4 **sweet potatoes**, about
   1.25 kg (2½ lb) in total,
   scrubbed
4 **boneless, skinless chicken
   thighs**, cut into chunks
1 **red onion**, cut into wedges
4 **plum tomatoes**, cut
   into chunks
150 g (5 oz) **chorizo
   sausage**, skinned and sliced
   or diced, if very large
leaves from 3 **rosemary
   sprigs**
4 tablespoons **olive oil**
salt and **pepper**

Cut the sweet potatoes in half, then into thick wedges and place in a large roasting tin with the chicken, onion and tomatoes. Tuck the chorizo in and around the potatoes, then sprinkle with the rosemary and some salt and pepper. Drizzle with the oil.

Roast in a preheated oven, 200°C (400°F), Gas Mark 6, for about 35 minutes, turning once or twice, until the chicken is golden and cooked through and the potato wedges are browned and tender.

Spoon on to warmed serving plates and serve with a watercress salad, if liked.

For mixed roots with fennel & chicken, use a mixture of 1.25 kg (2½ lb) baking potatoes, parsnips and carrots. Scrub the potatoes and peel the parsnips and carrots, then cut all the root vegetables into wedges. Add to the roasting tin with the chicken as above. Sprinkle with 2 teaspoons fennel seeds, 1 teaspoon ground turmeric and 1 teaspoon paprika, then drizzle with 4 tablespoons olive oil and roast as above.

turkey polpettes with tomatoes

Serves **4**
Preparation time **25 minutes**
Cooking time **30 minutes**

500 g (1 lb) **minced turkey**
2 **onions**, chopped
50 g (2 oz) **can anchovy fillets**, drained and chopped
50 g (2 oz) **fresh white breadcrumbs**
4 tablespoons **olive oil**
2 x 400 g (13 oz) **cans chopped tomatoes**
2 tablespoons **sun-dried tomato paste**
2 teaspoons **dried oregano**
1 tablespoon **light muscovado sugar**
125 g (4 oz) **pack mozzarella cheese**, drained and thinly sliced
salt and **pepper**

Mix together the turkey, one of the onions, the anchovies, breadcrumbs and a little salt and pepper in a bowl. Divide the mixture into 8 pieces and shape into flat patties.

Heat 2 tablespoons of the oil in a large frying pan and fry the patties for 8 minutes, until golden on both sides. Transfer to a plate. Add the remaining oil and onion to the pan and fry gently for 5 minutes. Stir in the tomatoes, tomato paste, oregano, sugar and a little salt and pepper and bring to a simmer.

Return the patties to the pan, pushing them down into the sauce. Cook gently, uncovered, for 15 minutes until the patties are cooked through.

Place the mozzarella slices on top and season with plenty of pepper. Cook under a preheated moderate grill until the cheese melts. Serve with warmed olive ciabatta, if liked.

For chicken escalopes with tomatoes & olives, halve 4 chicken breasts, about 125–150 g (4–5 oz) each, horizontally and place the slices between 2 sheets of clingfilm. Beat with a rolling pin to make thin escalopes. Season with salt and pepper. Cook the recipe as above using the chicken escalopes in place of the turkey polpettes and scattering the tomato mixture with 50 g (2 oz) chopped pitted black or green olives before adding the mozzarella.

caldo gallego

Serves **6**

Preparation time **30 minutes**, plus overnight soaking

Cooking time **2 hours 10 minutes**

1 **ham hock** or **gammon joint**, about 750 g (1½ lb)
150 g (5 oz) **dried haricot beans**
4 **chicken legs**
2 **onions**, chopped
3 **bay leaves**
1.2 litres (2 pints) **cold water**
500 g (1 lb) **floury potatoes**
1 tablespoon **ground paprika**
200 g (7 oz) **green cabbage**, shredded
15 g (½ oz) **fresh coriander**, roughly chopped
pepper

Soak the ham and beans in separate bowls of cold water overnight.

Drain the beans and transfer to a large saucepan. Cover with fresh cold water and bring to the boil. Reduce the heat and simmer for 40 minutes or until just tender. Drain and set aside.

Add the drained ham to the empty bean pan with the chicken legs, onions and bay leaves. Pour over the measurement water and bring to a gentle simmer. Cover and cook very gently for 1 hour.

Cut the potatoes into small chunks and add to the pan with the beans and paprika. Cook very gently, covered, for a further 20 minutes until the potatoes are tender.

Lift the chicken and ham from the pan. Once cool enough to handle, pull the meat from the bones, discarding the skin. Shred or chop all the meat into small pieces and return to the pan. Stir in the cabbage and coriander and heat through gently. Season with pepper and serve.

For hearty chicken broth, soak and then cook the beans as above. Omitting the ham, cook 6 chicken legs with the onions and bay leaves as above, also adding 3 large chopped carrots and 1 teaspoon caraway seeds. Then add 4 tablespoons finely chopped parsley and a little salt with the potatoes, beans and paprika, and continue as above.

quail with lentils & spiced pears

Serves **4**
Preparation time **15 minutes**
Cooking time **1¼ hours**

12 **shallots**
2 teaspoons **ground ginger**
½ teaspoon **chilli powder**
4 **plump quail**
40 g (1½ oz) **butter**
1 tablespoon **olive oil**
2 **ripe pears**, cored and cut
    into wedges
225 g (7½ oz) **dried**
    Puy lentils
1 **cinnamon stick**, halved
500 ml (17 fl oz) **chicken**
    stock (see page 36
    for homemade)
salt
watercress, to serve

Place the shallots in a heatproof bowl, cover with boiling water and leave to stand for 2 minutes. Drain and rinse in cold water. Peel away the skins, leaving the shallots whole.

Mix together the ginger, chilli powder and a little salt and rub all over the quail. Melt the butter with the oil in a flameproof casserole and fry the quail for 5 minutes, until browned on all sides. Drain to a plate.

Add the shallots and pears to the casserole, turning them in the butter for a few minutes until beginning to colour. Lift out the pears and set aside, then return the quail to the pan.

Rinse the lentils in cold water and tip around the quail. Add the cinnamon stick and stock and bring to a simmer. Cover and cook in a preheated oven, 180°C (350°F), Gas Mark 4, for 50 minutes until the quail are cooked through and the lentils are tender.

Stir the pears into the lentils and return to the oven for a further 10 minutes. Serve with watercress.

For creamy celeriac purée, to serve as an accompaniment, cut away the skin from a large celeriac and chop into large dice. Cut 400 g (13 oz) floury potatoes into similar-sized pieces. Place the vegetables in a large saucepan and cover with water. Season with a little salt and bring to the boil. Cook for about 20 minutes until the vegetables are tender. Drain well and return to the pan. Add 50 g (2 oz) butter, 100 ml (3½ fl oz) crème fraîche and plenty of pepper and mash well with a potato masher until smooth.

rabbit in white wine with rosemary

Serves **4–6**
Preparation time **15 minutes**
Cooking time **2 hours**

25 g (1 oz) **butter**
3 tablespoons **olive oil**
1 **rabbit**, about 1.5 kg (3 lb),
    jointed
2 **onions**, thinly sliced
1 **small celery stick**,
    finely diced
pinch of **dried chilli flakes**
3 **large rosemary sprigs**
1 **lemon**, quartered
12 **black olives**
350 ml (12 fl oz) **dry white
    wine**
250 ml (8 fl oz) **chicken stock**
    (see page 36 for homemade)
salt

Melt the butter with the oil in a large flameproof casserole with a tight-fitting lid large enough to hold the rabbit in a single layer. Season the rabbit pieces lightly with salt and add to the casserole with the onions, celery, chilli flakes and rosemary. Cover, reduce the heat to its lowest setting and cook for 1½ hours, turning the rabbit pieces every 30 minutes.

Remove the lid, increase the heat to high and boil for 15 minutes until most of the rabbit juices have evaporated. Add the lemon quarters and olives and stir well, then pour in the wine. Bring to the boil and boil for 2 minutes.

Add the stock and simmer, turning and basting the rabbit occasionally, for a further 10–12 minutes until the sauce is syrupy. Serve hot.

For chicken with olives & rosemary, replace the rabbit with 1 chicken, about 1.5 kg (3 lb), jointed (see page 12). Place the chicken with all the remaining ingredients above in a large roasting tin and cook in a preheated oven, 200°C (400°F), Gas Mark 6, for 1 hour, turning the chicken pieces occasionally, until the chicken is cooked through and tender and most of the juices have evaporated. Stir in 3 tablespoons double cream and serve immediately.

miso chicken broth

Serves **4**
Preparation time **10 minutes**
Cooking time **20 minutes**

1 tablespoon **sunflower oil**
2 **boneless, skinless chicken breasts**, diced
250 g (8 oz) **cup mushrooms**, trimmed and sliced
1 **carrot**, cut into thin matchsticks
1.5 cm (¾ inch) **piece of fresh root ginger**, grated
2 large pinches of **dried chilli flakes**
2 tablespoons **brown rice miso paste**
4 tablespoons **mirin** or **dry sherry**
2 tablespoons **light soy sauce**
1.2 litres (2 pints) **cold water**
2 **pak choi**, thinly sliced
4 **spring onions**, thinly sliced
4 tablespoons **chopped fresh coriander**

Heat the oil in a saucepan and fry the chicken for 5 minutes until golden on all sides. Add the mushrooms and carrot sticks, then the ginger, chilli flakes, miso paste, mirin or sherry and soy sauce.

Pour over the measurement water and bring to the boil, stirring. Reduce the heat and simmer for 10 minutes.

Add the pak choi, spring onions and coriander to the pan and cook for 2–3 minutes until the pak choi has just wilted. Spoon into bowls and serve immediately.

For hot & sour chicken soup, fry the chicken in the oil as above, then add 125 g (4 oz) trimmed and sliced mushrooms and 1 carrot, cut into matchsticks. Flavour with 2 finely chopped garlic cloves, 1 tablespoon red Thai curry paste, 1 tablespoon Thai fish sauce and 2 tablespoons light soy sauce. Add 1.2 litres (2 pints) chicken stock, bring to the boil and cook for 10 minutes. Add 125 g (4 oz) sliced baby corn and 50 g (2 oz) sliced mangetout with the spring onions and coriander as above and cook for 2–3 minutes. Ladle into bowls and serve with lime wedges.

pigeon with bacon & spelt

Serves **2**

Preparation time **15 minutes**,
plus marinating

Cooking time **40 minutes**

2 teaspoons **caster sugar**

2 teaspoons **salt**

4 **pigeon breasts**

25 g (1 oz) **butter**

1 **onion**, chopped

4 **smoked streaky bacon
rashers**, chopped

6 **tomatoes**, skinned (see
page 11) and roughly
chopped

2 tablespoons **balsamic
vinegar**

300 ml (½ pint) **chicken stock**
(see page 36 for homemade)

75 g (3 oz) **whole spelt**

5 g (¼ oz) **basil leaves**, torn
into pieces, plus extra to
garnish

salt and **pepper**

Mix the sugar with the salt and spread over the pigeon breasts. Place in a non-metallic bowl, cover loosely and leave to marinate in the refrigerator for 2–3 hours.

Wipe off the salt and sugar and pat the pigeon breasts dry with kitchen paper. Melt the butter in a large heavy-based frying pan and fry the pigeon breasts for 5 minutes until lightly browned on both sides. Drain to a plate and set aside.

Add the onion and bacon to the pan and fry gently for about 5 minutes until the bacon is beginning to crisp.

Stir in the tomatoes, vinegar, stock and spelt and bring to the boil. Reduce the heat, cover and cook gently for 25 minutes or until the spelt is just tender.

Cut the pigeon into slices, add to the pan with the basil and a little salt and pepper and heat through. Serve scattered with extra basil.

For pigeon with pickled walnut pilaf, marinate the pigeon breasts in the sugar and salt, then fry in the butter and lift out on to a plate as above. Fry the onion in the pan as above, adding 25 g (1 oz) flaked almonds and 2 crushed garlic cloves instead of the bacon. Add 125 g (4 oz) white long-grain rice, 200 ml (7 fl oz) chicken stock, ¼ teaspoon ground allspice and 25 g (1 oz) raisins. Cover and cook gently for 15–20 minutes until the rice is tender, adding a dash of water if the stock has been absorbed before the rice is cooked. Return the sliced pigeon to the pan with 3 chopped pickled walnuts and 3 tablespoons chopped fresh coriander. Season to taste with salt and pepper and serve.

chicken, chorizo & black bean stew

Serves **4–5**
Preparation time **15 minutes**,
  plus overnight soaking
Cooking time **2¼ hours**

250 g (8 oz) **dried**
  black beans
8 **bone-in, skinless**
  chicken thighs
150 g (5 oz) **chorizo**
  sausage, cut into
  small chunks
1 **onion**, sliced
1 **fennel bulb**, trimmed
  and chopped
2 **green peppers**, cored,
  deseeded and cut
  into chunks
1 teaspoon **saffron threads**
salt and **pepper**

Soak the beans in a bowl of cold water overnight. Drain and transfer to a large flameproof casserole. Cover with plenty of fresh cold water. Bring to the boil and boil for 10 minutes. Drain the beans and return to the pan.

Add the chicken, chorizo, onion, fennel and green peppers and sprinkle in the saffron. Almost cover the ingredients with cold water and bring to a simmer. Cover and cook in a preheated oven, 160°C (325°F), Gas Mark 3, for 2 hours or until the beans are very soft.

Drain a couple of spoonfuls of the beans with a large slotted spoon to a bowl and mash with a fork. Return to the casserole, stirring gently to thicken the juices. Season to taste with salt and pepper and serve.

For chorizo with chickpeas, fry 150 g (5 oz) diced chorizo in a large saucepan. Add 2 thinly sliced shallots, 2 x 400 g (13 oz) cans chopped tomatoes, 2 x 400 g (13 oz) cans chickpeas, 40 g (1½ oz) raisins, 2 tablespoons sherry vinegar, 1 tablespoon clear honey and 1 teaspoon ground paprika. Bring to a simmer, then reduce the heat, cover and cook gently for 30 minutes. Season to taste with salt and pepper and serve.

venison & pork meatballs

Serves **4**
Preparation time **30 minutes**
Cooking time **1½ hours**

400 g (13 oz) **minced venison**
200 g (7 oz) **minced pork**
2 teaspoons **chopped thyme**
3 tablespoons **olive oil**
1 **onion**, chopped
3 **carrots**, chopped
1 tablespoon **plain flour**
200 ml (7 fl oz) **beef stock** (see page 108 for homemade)
300 ml (½ pint) **red wine**
3 tablespoons **sun-dried tomato paste**
3 **bay leaves**
500 g (1 lb) **baby potatoes**, scrubbed
salt and **pepper**

Place the minced venison and pork, thyme and a little salt and pepper in a bowl and mix until well combined. Shape into 12 small balls about 3 cm (1¼ inches) in diameter.

Heat 2 tablespoons of the oil in a large heavy-based frying pan and fry the meatballs, half at a time, for 8–10 minutes until browned on all sides, lifting out with a slotted spoon on to a plate.

Add the remaining oil to the pan with the onion and carrots. Cook gently for 6–8 minutes until the vegetables have softened. Sprinkle in the flour and cook, stirring, for 1 minute. Remove from the heat and blend in the stock and wine. Stir in the tomato paste and bay leaves.

Bring to the boil, stirring, then reduce the heat to its lowest setting, cover with a lid or foil and cook gently for 10 minutes. Add the potatoes and meatballs to the pan, re-cover and cook for a further 50 minutes until the potatoes and meatballs are cooked through and tender. Check the seasoning and serve.

For merguez-spiced meatballs and squash, make and fry the meatballs as above, adding 2 teaspoons each lightly crushed cumin, coriander and fennel seeds and 2 teaspoons ground paprika instead of the thyme. Make the sauce as above, omitting the wine and using 500 ml (17 fl oz) beef stock. Replace the baby potatoes with 500 g (1 lb) skinned, deseeded and diced butternut squash and add 150 g (5 oz) sliced dried figs and 4 tablespoons chopped fresh coriander with the meatballs.

chicken with spring herbs

Serves **4**

Preparation time **15 minutes**

Cooking time **25 minutes**

250 g (8 oz) **mascarpone cheese**

1 handful of **chervil**, finely chopped

½ bunch of **parsley**, finely chopped

2 tablespoons **chopped mint leaves**

4 **boneless, skin-on chicken breasts**

25 g (1 oz) **butter**

200 ml (7 fl oz) **white wine**

salt and **pepper**

Mix together the mascarpone and herbs in a bowl and season well with salt and pepper. Lift the skin away from each chicken breast and spread a quarter of the mascarpone mixture on each breast. Replace the skin and smooth carefully over the mascarpone mixture. Season with salt and pepper.

Place the chicken in a baking dish, dot with the butter and pour the wine around it.

Roast the chicken in a preheated oven, 180°C (350°F), Gas Mark 4, for 20–25 minutes until golden and crisp and cooked through. Serve with garlic bread, if liked.

For baby glazed carrots, to serve as an alternative accompaniment to the garlic bread, melt 25 g (1 oz) butter in a saucepan, add 500 g (1 lb) young carrots, quartered lengthways, a pinch of caster sugar and salt and pepper to taste. Pour over just enough water to cover and simmer gently for 15–20 minutes until the carrots are tender and the liquid has evaporated, adding 2 tablespoons orange juice towards the end of the cooking time. Serve with the chicken garnished with chopped parsley.

meat

lamb with broad beans & fennel

Serves **4**
Preparation time **10 minutes**
Cooking time **2¾ hours**

1 kg (2 lb) **lamb fillet**
50 g (2 oz) **fresh white breadcrumbs**
2 small **fennel bulbs**, trimmed and cut into thin wedges
200 g (7 oz) **podded broad beans**
finely grated rind of 1 **lemon**, plus 1 tablespoon **juice**
25 g (1 oz) **chopped parsley**, plus extra to garnish
4 **garlic cloves**, crushed
3 tablespoons **extra virgin olive oil**
100 ml (3½ fl oz) **dry white wine** or **chicken stock** (see page 36 for homemade)
2 tablespoons **black treacle**
salt and **pepper**
olive ciabatta, to serve

Cut the lamb fillet into 5 cm (2 inch) lengths, discarding any areas of excess fat. Place in a large bowl and add the breadcrumbs, fennel, broad beans, lemon rind, parsley and garlic. Mix the ingredients together well and turn into a casserole.

Mix the olive oil with the wine or stock, lemon juice and treacle and drizzle over the meat.

Cover the casserole and cook in a preheated oven, 200°C (400°F), Gas Mark 6, for 45 minutes.

Reduce the oven temperature to 160°C (325°F), Gas Mark 3. Turn the ingredients in the casserole, re-cover and return to the oven for a further 2 hours. Season to taste with salt and pepper and sprinkle with extra parsley. Serve with warmed olive ciabatta.

For cannellini & potato mash, to serve as an alternative accompaniment to the ciabatta, cook 500 g (1 lb) potatoes in a saucepan of lightly salted boiling water until tender. Drain, reserving a ladleful of the cooking water. Return the potatoes to the pan with the reserved water and 2 x 400 g (13 oz) cans cannellini beans, drained, and 1 tablespoon chopped young thyme leaves. Mash well with a potato masher until smooth. Beat in 5 tablespoons extra virgin olive oil and serve hot.

spiced steak & pepper wraps

Serves **6**
Preparation time **20 minutes**,
plus marinating
Cooking time **35 minutes**

750 g (1½ lb) **beef skirt**
(from the rump end) or
rump steak
1 teaspoon **dried oregano**
2 teaspoons **cumin seeds**
2 teaspoons **caster sugar**
2 **garlic cloves**, crushed
finely grated rind and juice
of **1 lime**
4 tablespoons **vegetable oil**
2 **red onions,** thinly sliced
2 **red peppers**, cored,
deseeded and thinly sliced
2 **orange** or **yellow peppers**,
cored, deseeded and
thinly sliced
6 **wheat tortillas**, warmed
2 **Little Gem lettuce**,
shredded

To serve
soured cream
sweet chilli sauce

Cut the beef into 1 cm (½ inch) wide strips, discarding any areas of excess fat. Place in a non-metallic bowl.

Crush the oregano and cumin seeds using a pestle and mortar and mix with the sugar, garlic and lime rind and juice. Add to the beef and mix until well combined. Cover loosely and leave to marinate in the refrigerator for 1 hour.

Heat the oil in a frying pan or wok and fry the onions and peppers, stirring frequently, for 20 minutes until very soft and beginning to colour. Drain the vegetables to a plate and wipe out the pan. Fry the beef, in batches, for 5–8 minutes per batch, turning, in the remaining oil until golden on all sides, adding the cooked meat to the plate. Return the peppers, onions and meat to the pan and heat through briefly. Add any marinade left in the bowl and cook, stirring, for about 5 minutes until browned.

Serve on the warmed tortillas with the lettuce, along with soured cream and sweet chilli sauce.

For avocado relish, to serve as an additional accompaniment, stone and peel 2 ripe avocados, then finely chop. Skin (see page 11) and scoop the seeds from 2 small tomatoes, then finely chop the flesh. Mix in a bowl with the avocado, 1 finely chopped spring onion, the finely grated rind and juice of 1 lime, 2 teaspoons caster sugar, 3 tablespoons finely chopped fresh coriander and a little salt and pepper. Stir together and transfer to a serving dish.

pork & leek stew with dumplings

Serves **4–5**
Preparation time **25 minutes**
Cooking time **2 hours**

1 kg (2 lb) **boneless lean pork**, diced
2 tablespoons **vegetable oil**
1 large **onion**, chopped
500 g (1 lb) **leeks**, trimmed, cleaned and chopped
3 **bay leaves**
1.5 litres (2½ pints) **beef** or **chicken stock** (see pages 108 and 36 for homemade)
75 g (3 oz) **pearl barley**
150 g (5 oz) **self-raising flour**
75 g (3 oz) **beef** or **vegetable suet**
about 125 ml (4 fl oz) **cold water**
150 g (5 oz) **stoned prunes**, halved
salt and **pepper**

Season the pork well, with salt and pepper. Heat 1 tablespoon of the oil in a large flameproof casserole and fry the pork in batches until browned on all sides, lifting out with a slotted spoon on to a plate. Add the remaining oil to the casserole and gently fry the onion and leeks for 5 minutes.

Return the pork to the casserole, add the bay leaves and stock and bring to a simmer. Stir in the pearl barley. Cover, reduce the heat to its lowest setting and cook for about 1½ hours until the pork and barley are tender and the cooking juices have thickened.

Mix together the flour, suet and a little salt and pepper in a bowl. Add the measurement water and mix with a round-bladed knife to a soft dough, adding a dash more water if the mixture feels dry and crumbly, but don't make it too sticky.

Stir the prunes into the stew and season to taste with salt and pepper. Using a dessertspoon, place spoonfuls of the dumpling mixture on the surface of the stew, spacing them slightly apart. Re cover and cook gently for a further 15–20 minutes until the dumplings have risen and have a fluffy texture. Serve in shallow bowls.

For Irish champ, to serve as an alternative accompaniment to the dumplings, cook 1.25 kg (2½ lb) floury potatoes in a large saucepan of lightly salted boiling water until tender. Drain, return to the pan and mash with a potato masher until smooth. Finely chop 1 bunch of spring onions and add to the pan with 50 g (2 oz) butter, 200 ml (7 fl oz) milk and plenty of pepper. Beat well, check and adjust the seasoning and serve.

oxtail stew with star anise

Serves **4**
Preparation time **20 minutes**
Cooking time **3¾ hours**

2 tablespoons **plain flour**
2 kg (4 lb) **oxtail**
3 tablespoons **vegetable oil**
2 **onions**, chopped
2 **celery sticks**, chopped
5 **star anise**
50 g (2 oz) **fresh root ginger**,
    peeled and finely chopped
800 ml (1 pint 7fl oz) **beef** or
    chicken stock (see pages
    108 and 36 for homemade)
200 g (7 oz) **can chopped
    tomatoes**
finely grated rind and juice of
    1 **orange**
2 tablespoons **soy sauce**
4 tablespoons **chopped fresh
    coriander**, plus extra to
    garnish
salt and **pepper**

Season the flour with salt and pepper on a plate. Coat the oxtail with the flour.

Heat the oil in a flameproof casserole and fry the oxtail in batches until browned on all sides, lifting out with a slotted spoon on to a plate. Add the onions and celery to the casserole and fry gently for 5 minutes. Add the star anise, ginger and any flour left over from coating, and cook, stirring, for 1 minute.

Blend in the stock, tomatoes, orange rind and juice and soy sauce. Return the oxtail to the pan and bring to a simmer, stirring. Cover and cook in a preheated oven, 150°C (300°F), Gas Mark 2, for about 3½ hours or until the meat falls easily from the bone.

Fold in the coriander and season to taste with salt and pepper. Serve garnished with extra coriander.

For beery oxtail stew, make the stew as above, adding 2 chopped carrots when frying the vegetables and omitting the star anise and ginger. Replace half the stock with 500 ml (17 fl oz) strong ale and the tomatoes, orange, soy sauce and coriander with 4 tablespoons tomato purée, 2 tablespoons black treacle, 2 tablespoons Worcestershire sauce and 4 tablespoons chopped parsley.

beef, pickled onion & beer stew

Serves **4**
Preparation time **10 minutes**
Cooking time **2¼ hours**

3 tablespoons **plain flour**
1 kg (2 lb) **braising steak**
2 tablespoons **olive oil**
500 g (1 lb) **jar pickled onions, drained**
2 **carrots**, thickly sliced
300 ml (½ pint) **beer**
600 ml (1 pint) **beef stock** (see page 108 for homemade)
4 tablespoons **tomato purée**
1 tablespoon **Worcestershire sauce**
2 **bay leaves**
salt and **pepper**
chopped parsley, to garnish

Season the flour with salt and pepper on a plate. Cut the beef into large chunks and coat with the flour.

Heat the oil in a large flameproof casserole and fry the beef in batches until browned on all sides, lifting out with a slotted spoon on to a plate. Return all the beef to the casserole.

Stir the pickled onions and carrots into the casserole, then gradually blend in the beer and stock. Bring to the boil, stirring, then add the tomato purée, Worcestershire sauce, bay leaves and salt and pepper to taste.

Cover and cook in a preheated oven, 160°C (325°F), Gas Mark 3, for 2 hours, stirring halfway through, until the beef and vegetables are tender. Garnish with chopped parsley and serve immediately.

For soft Parmesan polenta, to serve as an accompaniment, bring 1 litre (1¾ pints) water to the boil with 2 teaspoons salt in a saucepan. Add 175 g (6 oz) polenta in a stream, whisking constantly to avoid lumps forming. Once it starts to thicken, use a wooden spoon to stir the polenta while it cooks for 5 minutes. Remove from the heat and stir in 50 g (2 oz) butter and 4 tablespoons freshly grated Parmesan cheese. Season to taste with salt and pepper and serve immediately.

veal with orzo

Serves **4**
Preparation time **15 minutes**
Cooking time **25 minutes**

625 g (1 ¼ lb) **veal escalopes**
4 tablespoons **olive oil**
1 large **onion**, finely chopped
4 **garlic cloves**, crushed
500 g (1 lb) **ripe tomatoes**,
  skinned (see page 11) and
  roughly chopped
750 ml (1 ¼ pints) **chicken
  stock** (see page 36
  for homemade)
250 ml (8 fl oz) **passata**
4 tablespoons **sun-dried
  tomato paste**
2 tablespoons **finely chopped
  oregano**
250 g (8 oz) **dried orzo pasta**
100 g (3 ½ oz) **feta cheese**,
  crumbled
salt and **pepper**

Cut the veal escalopes into pieces about 5 cm
(2 inches) across. Season on both sides with salt
and pepper.

Heat the oil in a flameproof casserole and quickly fry
the veal pieces in two batches for 5 minutes, until lightly
browned on both sides, lifting out with a slotted spoon
on to a plate. Add the onion to the casserole and fry
gently for 5 minutes until softened. Stir in the garlic and
fry for 1 minute.

Add the tomatoes to the casserole with the stock,
passata, tomato paste and oregano. Bring to the
boil and stir in the orzo. Reduce the heat and cook,
stirring frequently, for 6–8 minutes or until the pasta
has softened.

Return the veal to the casserole and season to taste
with salt and pepper. Cook for 2 minutes. Scatter the
feta over the meat before serving.

For garlic & saffron alioli, to serve as an alternative
accompaniment to the feta topping, place ½ teaspoon
crumbled saffron threads in a bowl with 1 tablespoon
boiling water. Leave to stand for 2 minutes. Crush
1 plump garlic clove and mix with 125 g (4 oz)
mayonnaise in a separate bowl. Stir in the saffron
and liquid and season lightly with salt and pepper.
Turn into a small bowl and serve spooned over the veal.

irish lamb & potato stew

Serves **4–5**
Preparation time **20 minutes**
Cooking time **2¾ hours**

1 kg (2 lb) **lamb chump
chops** or **lamb fillet**
2 tablespoons **vegetable oil**
400 g (13 oz) **carrots**, sliced
3 **onions**, chopped
1 **leek**, trimmed, cleaned and
thinly sliced
750 g (1½ lb) **floury
potatoes**, cut into large
chunks
3 **bay leaves**
50 g (2 oz) **pearl barley**
1 litre (1¾ pints) **lamb** or
chicken stock (see pages
110 and 36 for homemade)
4 tablespoons **chopped
parsley**
4 tablespoons **chopped
chives**
salt and **pepper**

Cut the lamb into chunky pieces and season with salt and pepper.

Heat the oil in a flameproof casserole or large saucepan and fry the lamb in batches until browned on all sides, lifting out with a slotted spoon on to a plate.

Layer up the lamb, carrots, onions, leek and potatoes in the pan. Add the bay leaves and sprinkle in the pearl barley.

Pour the stock over all the ingredients and bring to a simmer. Cover, reduce the heat to its lowest setting and cook for 2½ hours or until the lamb is meltingly tender.

Stir in the parsley and chives and cook for a further 10 minutes. Season to taste with salt and pepper and serve.

For lamb stew with spring vegetables, fry the lamb, then layer up in the casserole or saucepan with the onions, leek and potatoes, cover with the stock and cook for 2 hours as above. Stir in 400 g (13 oz) scrubbed baby carrots, 200 g (7 oz) podded baby broad beans and 2 tablespoons chopped mint, then re-cover and cook for a further 30 minutes. Finally, add 150 g (5 oz) trimmed asparagus spears and cook for a further 5 minutes.

mediterranean pork casserole

Serves **2**
Preparation time **10 minutes**
Cooking time **1 hour 10 minutes**

1 tablespoon **olive oil**
250 g (8 oz) **boneless lean pork**, cut into chunks
1 **red onion**, cut into thin wedges
1 **garlic clove**, crushed
1 **yellow pepper**, cored, deseeded and chopped
8 **artichoke hearts in oil**, drained and quartered
200 g (7 oz) **can chopped tomatoes**
1 small glass **red wine**
50 g (2 oz) **black olives**
grated rind of 1 **lemon**
1 **bay leaf**
1 **thyme sprig**, plus extra to garnish
garlic bread, to serve

Heat the oil in a flameproof casserole and fry the pork for 4–5 minutes until browned on all sides. Lift out with a slotted spoon on to a plate.

Add the onion, garlic and yellow pepper to the casserole and fry for 2 minutes. Return the pork to the casserole together with all the remaining ingredients.

Bring to the boil, then reduce the heat, cover and cook gently for 1 hour or until the meat is tender. Garnish with thyme and serve with garlic bread.

For borlotti bean casserole, omit the pork and fry the onion, garlic and yellow pepper in the oil as above, then stir in the artichoke hearts and tomatoes. Rinse and drain a 400 g (13 oz) can borlotti beans and add to the casserole with the wine, olives, lemon rind and herbs. Bring to the boil, then reduce the heat, cover and cook gently for about 1 hour. Serve garnished with chopped parsley.

kleftiko

Serves **4**
Preparation time **15 minutes**
Cooking time **2 hours
5 minutes**

8 **lamb loin chops**
1 tablespoon **olive oil**
2 **onions**, thinly sliced
2 tablespoons **chopped
oregano**
finely grated rind and juice of
1 lemon
1 **cinnamon stick**, halved
2 **tomatoes**, skinned (see
page 11) and thinly sliced
500 g (1 lb) **waxy potatoes**,
cut into small chunks
150 ml (¼ pint) **lamb** or
chicken stock (see pages
110 and 36 for homemade)
salt and **pepper**

Season the chops on both sides with salt and pepper. Heat the oil in a shallow flameproof casserole with a tight-fitting lid and fry the chops for 5 minutes until browned on both sides.

Scatter the onions into the casserole and add the oregano, lemon rind and juice and cinnamon. Tuck the tomatoes and potatoes around the lamb and add the stock and a little salt and pepper.

Cover and bake in a preheated oven, 160°C (325°F), Gas Mark 3, for 2 hours or until the lamb is very tender. Serve with warmed Greek bread.

For lamb chilli with potatoes, heat 2 tablespoons olive oil in a saucepan and fry 500 g (1 lb) minced lamb with 1 chopped onion, 1 teaspoon crushed cumin seeds and ½ teaspoon dried chilli flakes, breaking up the mince with a wooden spoon, for 8 minutes until lightly browned. Add a 400 g (13 oz) can plum tomatoes, 2 teaspoons light muscovado sugar and 450 ml (¾ pint) lamb or chicken stock. Bring to a simmer, then reduce the heat, cover and cook very gently for 15 minutes. Stir in a drained 400 g (13 oz) can red kidney beans, 250 g (8 oz) scrubbed and diced new potatoes and 3 tablespoons chopped fresh coriander. Re-cover and cook for a further 25 minutes or until the potatoes are tender. Check the seasoning and serve.

calves' liver & caramelized onions

Serves **4**
Preparation time **10 minutes**
Cooking time **40–45 minutes**

50 g (2 oz) **butter**
2 tablespoons **olive oil**
2 **large onions**, thinly sliced
625 g (1¼ 1b) **calves' liver**,
    thinly sliced (ask your
    butcher to slice as thinly
    as possible)
2 tablespoons finely chopped
    flat leaf parsley
salt and **pepper**

Melt half the butter with the oil in a large heavy-based frying pan with a tight-fitting lid. Add the onions and season with salt and pepper, then cover, reduce the heat to its lowest setting and cook, stirring occasionally, for 35–40 minutes until very soft and golden.

Lift the onions out with a slotted spoon into a bowl and increase the heat under the pan to high.

Season the liver with salt and pepper. Melt the remaining butter in the pan. Once the butter starts foaming, add the liver and cook for 1–2 minutes until browned. Turn over and return the onions to the pan. Cook for a further 1 minute. Serve scattered with the parsley.

For chicken livers & caramelized onions, cook the onions as above and lift from the pan. Instead of the calves' liver, use 400 g (13 oz) chicken livers. Season 2 tablespoons plain flour with salt and pepper on a plate and coat the livers with the flour. Cook the livers in the remaining butter in the pan as above for 4–5 minutes, turning once. Add 1 tablespoon aged balsamic vinegar and swirl in the pan for a couple of seconds, then return the caramelized onions to the pan. Cook for a further 1 minute, then stir in the parsley as above and serve immediately.

pork cheek mushroom casserole

Serves **5–6**
Preparation time **20 minutes**
Cooking time **2¾ hours**

3 tablespoons **plain flour**
1 kg (2 lb) **pork cheeks**
50 g (2 oz) **butter**
1 tablespoon **vegetable oil**
300 g (10 oz) **chestnut
   mushrooms**, trimmed
   and sliced
2 **onions**, chopped
350 ml (12 fl oz) **cider**
300 ml (½ pint) **pork** or
   chicken stock (see page 36
   for homemade)
2 tablespoons chopped
   tarragon
2 tablespoons **grainy mustard**
4 tablespoons **double cream**
salt and **pepper**

Season the flour with salt and pepper on a plate. Cut the pork cheeks into chunks and coat with the flour.

Melt half the butter with the oil in a flameproof casserole and fry the pork in batches until browned on all sides, lifting out with a slotted spoon on to a plate. Melt the remaining butter in the casserole and fry the mushrooms for 5 minutes, until all their juices have evaporated and they are pale golden. Lift out on to a separate plate and set aside.

Return the pork to the casserole with any flour left over from coating and cook, stirring, for 1 minute. Stir in the onions, then blend in the cider and stock. Bring to the boil, stirring, then cover and cook in a preheated oven, 150°C (300°F), Gas Mark 2, for 2½ hours or until the meat is very tender, adding the tarragon and mustard halfway through cooking.

Return the mushrooms to the casserole and stir in the cream. Heat through gently, season to taste with salt and pepper and serve.

For beef & ale casserole, cut 1 kg (2 lb) braising steak into large pieces, discarding any areas of excess fat. Make the casserole as above using the beef instead of the pork and 350 ml (12 fl oz) strong ale in place of the cider. Add the mustard with 1 tablespoon chopped thyme instead of the tarragon, then finish with the cream as above.

lamb tagine with butter beans

Serves **4**
Preparation time **15 minutes**
Cooking time **1¼ hours**

700 g (1 lb 6 oz) **lamb fillet**
4 tablespoons **olive oil**
2 **red onions**, thinly sliced
2 **garlic cloves**, crushed
1 teaspoon **ground turmeric**
1 teaspoon **ground ginger**
1 teaspoon **ground cinnamon**
150 ml (¼ pint) **lamb** or
   chicken stock (see pages
   110 and 36 for homemade)
2 tablespoons **clear honey**
2 ready-made or homemade
   preserved lemons
   (see below)
100 g (3½ oz) **pitted black
   olives**
2 x 400 g (13 oz) **cans butter
   beans**, rinsed and drained
15 g (½ oz) **chopped parsley**,
   plus extra to garnish
salt and **pepper**

Cut the lamb into 5 cm (2 inch) pieces, discarding any areas of excess fat. Season with salt and pepper.

Heat the oil in a flameproof casserole and fry the lamb, half at a time, until browned on all sides, lifting out with a slotted spoon on to a plate. Add the onions to the casserole and fry for 5 minutes until softened. Add the garlic and spices and cook, stirring, for 1 minute.

Stir the stock and honey into the casserole and bring to a simmer. Return the lamb to the pan, cover and cook in a preheated oven, 160°C (325°F), Gas Mark 3, for 40 minutes. Meanwhile, halve the preserved lemons and discard the pulp. Finely chop the rind.

Add the preserved lemon rind to the casserole with the olives, beans and parsley. Return to the oven for a further 20 minutes. Season to taste with salt and pepper, garnish with extra parsley and serve with warmed flatbreads, if liked.

For homemade preserved lemons, wash and dry 3 small unwaxed lemons. Cut lengthways into 8 wedges keeping them intact at one end. Measure 3 tablespoons sea salt and sprinkle the cut sides of the lemons with 2 tablespoons of the measured salt. Pack the lemons into a thoroughly clean clip-top preserving jar in which they fit quite snugly. Tuck a couple of bay leaves into the jar and add the remaining salt. Squeeze the juice from a further 2 lemons and pour into the jar. Top up with cold water until the lemons are completely covered. Tap the jar to remove any air bubbles. Store for a least 2 weeks before use.

pork chops baked with potatoes

Serves **4**
Preparation time **10 minutes**
Cooking time **50 minutes**

2 tablespoons **olive oil**
4 **large pork chops**, about
   250 g (8 oz) each
125 g (4 oz) **smoked bacon**
   in one piece, rind discarded,
   diced
1 **large onion**, sliced
750 g (1½ lb) **potatoes**, cut
   into 2.5 cm (1 in) cubes
2 **garlic cloves**, chopped
2 teaspoons **dried oregano**
grated rind and juice of
   1 **lemon**
250 ml (8 fl oz) **chicken stock**
   (see page 36 for homemade)
salt and **pepper**
thyme leaves, to garnish
   (optional)

Heat the oil in an ovenproof frying pan or flameproof casserole and fry the pork chops until browned on both sides. Lift out with a slotted spoon on to a plate.

Add the bacon and onion to the pan and cook over a medium heat, stirring, for 3–4 minutes until golden.

Stir the potatoes, garlic, oregano and lemon rind into the pan. Pour over the stock and lemon juice and season lightly with salt and pepper. Cook, uncovered, in a preheated oven, 180°C (350°F), Gas Mark 4, for 20 minutes.

Arrange the chops on top of the potato mixture and return to the oven for a further 20 minutes or until the potatoes and pork chops are cooked through. Serve garnished with thyme leaves, if liked.

For pork chops with sweet potatoes & sage, cook the recipe above using 750 g (1½ lb) sweet potatoes, peeled and cut into cubes, instead of the potatoes and 1 tablespoon chopped sage in place of the dried oregano.

beef, beetroot & red cabbage

Serves **6**
Preparation time **25 minutes**
Cooking time **2¾ hours**

2 teaspoons **pepper**
2 tablespoons **plain flour**
1 kg (2 lb) **beef skirt**
2 tablespoons **olive oil**
100 g (3½ oz) **streaky bacon**, chopped
2 **onions**, sliced
300 ml (½ pint) **red wine**
300 ml (½ pint) **beef stock** (see page 108 for homemade)
4 tablespoons **sun-dried tomato paste**
2 teaspoons **caraway seeds**
600 g (1 lb 3 oz) **beetroot**, scrubbed and cut into thin wedges
400 g (13 oz) **red cabbage**, sliced
3 tablespoons **balsamic vinegar**
salt
soured cream and **grainy bread**, to serve

Mix the pepper into the flour with a little salt on a plate. Cut the beef into large chunks, about 5 cm (2 inches) across, and coat with the flour.

Heat 2 tablespoons of the oil in a flameproof casserole and fry the beef in batches until browned on all sides, lifting out with a slotted spoon on to a plate.

Add the bacon and onions to the casserole and fry gently for 6–8 minutes until beginning to colour. Add any flour left over from coating and cook, stirring, for 1 minute.

Blend in the wine and stock, then return the beef to the pan with the tomato paste and caraway seeds. Bring to a simmer, stirring, then cover and cook in a preheated oven, 150°C (300°F), Gas Mark 2, for 1 hour.

Stir the beetroot, red cabbage and balsamic vinegar into the casserole and return to the oven for a further 1½ hours or until the meat and vegetables are very tender. Add a little salt if necessary and serve in bowls with soured cream and warmed grainy bread.

For creamy horseradish mash, to serve as an accompaniment, cook 1.25 kg (2½ lb) floury potatoes in a large saucepan of salted boiling water for 20 minutes or until tender. Drain and return to the pan. Dot 50 g (2 oz) butter into the potatoes with 100 ml (3½ fl oz) crème fraîche and 4 tablespoons hot horseradish sauce. Mash well with a potato masher until smooth.

asian pork with water chestnuts

Serves **4**
Preparation time **20 minutes**,
  plus marinating
Cooking time **10 minutes**

500 g (1 lb) **pork fillet**
5 tablespoons **soy sauce**
1 teaspoon **Chinese five-spice powder**
2 tablespoons **clear honey**
1 teaspoon **cornflour**
3 tablespoons **cold water**
2 tablespoons **stir-fry** or **wok oil** or **vegetable oil**
300 g (10 oz) **pak choi,** shredded
1 bunch of **spring onions,** cut into 1.5 cm (¾ inch) lengths
25 g (1 oz) piece of **fresh root ginger,** peeled and finely chopped
1 **hot red chilli,** deseeded and thinly sliced
3 **garlic cloves,** thinly sliced
75 g (3 oz) **canned water chestnuts,** drained and halved
300 g (10 oz) **straight-to-wok fine noodles**

Cut the pork fillet in half lengthways, then across into very thin slices, discarding any areas of excess fat. Place in a bowl and drizzle with 2 tablespoons of the soy sauce, the five-spice powder and honey. Mix well, cover and marinate in a cool place for 30 minutes.

Mix the cornflour with the measurement water in a cup until smooth. Stir in the remaining soy sauce.

Heat 1 tablespoon of the oil in a wok or large frying pan over a high heat. Add the pak choi and spring onions and stir-fry for a couple of minutes until the greens have wilted. Lift out on to a plate. Add the remaining oil to the pan, tip in the pork and fry, turning once, for 3 minutes or until cooked through. Add the ginger, chilli and garlic and cook for a further 1 minute.

Return the vegetables to the pan with the water chestnuts, noodles and soy sauce mixture. Cook, stirring constantly, for 2–3 minutes until hot and the sauce is thickened and glossy. Serve immediately.

For easy pork & noodle soup, prepare the pork and marinate it as above. Heat 1 tablespoon wok or vegetable oil in a wok or saucepan and fry the pork, turning the pieces during cooking, for 3 minutes until golden. Add 750 ml (1¼ pints) pork or chicken stock, 25 g (1 oz) fresh root ginger, peeled and shredded, and a good pinch of dried chilli flakes. Cover and cook gently for 15 minutes until the pork is tender. Add 300 g (10 oz) straight-to-wok fine noodles, 200 g (7 oz) frozen peas, 40 g (1½ oz) finely chopped fresh coriander, 2 more tablespoons soy sauce and 1 teaspoon rice vinegar. Heat gently for 2–3 minutes.

braised beef with pickled walnuts

Serves **4**
Preparation time **20 minutes**
Cooking time **2½ hours**

2 tablespoons **plain flour**
1 kg (2 lb) **braising** or **chuck steak** in one piece
2 tablespoons **olive oil**
2 **onions**, chopped
3 **celery sticks**, sliced
3 **bay leaves**
several **rosemary sprigs**
2 **garlic cloves**, crushed
450 ml (¾ pint) **beef stock** (see page 108 for homemade)
125 g (4 oz) **walnuts**, chopped and lightly toasted
125 g (4 oz) **pickled walnuts**, drained and roughly chopped
2 tablespoons **grainy mustard**
5 tablespoons **chopped parsley**, plus extra to garnish
salt and **pepper**
steamed green beans, to serve

Season the flour with salt and pepper on a plate. Coat the beef with the flour.

Heat the oil in a flameproof casserole and fry the beef in batches until browned on all sides, turning it slowly in the oil. Transfer to a plate. Add the onions and celery to the casserole and fry gently for 6–8 minutes until softened.

Tip any flour left over from coating into the casserole and cook, stirring, for 1 minute. Push the vegetables to one side and return the beef to the centre of the pan. Add the bay leaves, rosemary, garlic and stock. Bring to a simmer, stirring, then cover and cook in a preheated oven, 150°C (300°F), Gas Mark 2, for 1½ hours.

Stir all the walnuts, the mustard and parsley into the casserole, re-cover and return to the oven for a further 45 minutes. Season to taste with salt and pepper and serve with steamed green beans garnished with parsley.

For braised lambs' liver with pickled walnuts, cut 500 g (1 lb) lambs' liver into large pieces and coat in 2 teaspoons plain flour seasoned with salt and pepper. Melt 25 g (1 oz) butter with 2 tablespoons olive oil in a saucepan and fry the liver briefly until lightly browned. Lift out with a slotted spoon on to a plate. Add 2 sliced onions to the pan and fry until soft and browned. Return the liver to the pan with 150 ml (¼ pint) chicken stock, 2 teaspoons grainy mustard and 50 g (2 oz) each chopped toasted walnuts and drained pickled walnuts. Heat through gently and season to taste with salt and pepper before serving.

sri lankan-style lamb curry

Serves **4**

Preparation time **10 minutes**

Cooking time about **35 minutes**

500 g (1 lb) **boneless shoulder** or **leg of lamb**, diced

2 **potatoes**, cut into large chunks

4 tablespoons **olive oil**

400 g (13 oz) **can chopped tomatoes**

150 ml (¼ pint) **water**

salt and **pepper**

Curry paste

1 **onion**, grated

1 tablespoon peeled and finely chopped **fresh root ginger**

1 teaspoon finely chopped **garlic**

½ teaspoon **ground turmeric**

1 teaspoon **ground coriander**

½ teaspoon **ground cumin**

½ teaspoon **fennel seeds**

½ teaspoon **cumin seeds**

3 **cardamom pods**, crushed

2 **green chillies**, finely diced

5 cm (2 inch) **cinnamon stick**

2 **lemon grass stalks**, thinly sliced

Make the curry paste. Mix together all the ingredients in a large bowl. (For a milder curry, remove the seeds from the chillies before dicing.) Add the lamb and potatoes and mix well.

Heat the oil in a heavy-based saucepan or flameproof casserole, tip in the lamb and potato mixture and cook, stirring, for 6–8 minutes.

Stir in the tomatoes and measurement water and bring to the boil. Season well with salt and pepper, then reduce the heat and simmer for 20–25 minutes until the potatoes are cooked and the lamb is tender. Serve with toasted naan breads and a bowl of Greek yogurt, if liked.

For beef & potato curry, use 500 g (1 lb) rump steak, cut into chunks, instead of the lamb. Cook the recipe as above and then serve with a generous sprinkling of chopped fresh coriander.

steak & kidney hotpot

Serves **4**
Preparation time **30 minutes**
Cooking time **2¼ hours**

210 g (7½ oz) **plain flour**,
   plus extra for dusting
750g (1½ lb) **braising steak**,
   cut into chunks
150 g (5 oz) **lambs' kidneys**,
   cut into small pieces
3 tablespoons **vegetable oil**
2 **onions**, chopped
600 ml (1 pint) **beef
   stock** (see page 108
   for homemade)
½ teaspoon **baking powder**
100 g (3½ oz) **beef suet**
about 150 ml (¼ pint)
   cold water
85 g (3¼ oz) **can smoked
   oysters**, drained and halved
3 tablespoons chopped
   parsley
3 tablespoons **Worcestershire
   sauce**
beaten egg, to glaze
salt and **pepper**

Season 1½ tablespoons of the flour on a plate. Coat the beef and kidneys with the flour. Heat 2 tablespoons of the oil in a flameproof casserole and fry the meat in batches until browned on all sides, lifting out with a slotted spoon on to a plate.

Heat the remaining oil in the casserole and fry the onions for 5 minutes. Tip in any flour left over from coating. Cook, stirring, for 1 minute. Blend in the stock.

Return all the meat to the casserole and bring to a simmer, stirring. Cover and cook in a preheated oven, 160°C (325°F), Gas Mark 3, for 1½ hours.

Mix together the remaining flour, baking powder, suet and a little salt and pepper in a bowl. Add enough of the measurement water, mixing with a round-bladed knife, to make a soft dough. Roll the dough out on a floured surface to a round the same diameter as the casserole.

Stir the oysters, parsley and Worcestershire sauce into the casserole and increase the oven temperature to 200°C (400°F), Gas Mark 6. Lay the pastry dough over the filling and brush with beaten egg to glaze. Bake for about 25 minutes until the pastry is pale golden.

For steak & mushroom pie, make the steak and kidney mixture as above, adding 150 g (5 oz) trimmed button mushrooms instead of the oysters. Once cooked, leave to cool. Roll out 350 g (11½ oz) ready-made puff pastry on a lightly floured surface until a little larger than the diameter of the casserole. Lay the pastry over the filling, pressing it against the dish. Brush with beaten egg and bake in a preheated oven, 220°C (425°F), Gas Mark 7, for 30 minutes or until risen and golden.

pork saltado

Serves **4**
Preparation time **20 minutes**
Cooking time **45 minutes**

3 **garlic cloves**, crushed
1 **red chilli,** deseeded and
  finely chopped
4 tablespoons **soy sauce**
1½ teaspoons lightly crushed
  coriander seeds
1½ teaspoons lightly crushed
  cumin seeds
1 tablespoon **white wine**
  vinegar
750 g (1½ lb) **pork fillet**, cut
  into 1.5 cm (¾ inch) pieces
5 tablespoons **vegetable oil**
750 g (1½ lb) **potatoes**, cut
  into 1.5 cm (¾ inch) pieces
4 **red onions**, sliced
500 g (1 lb) **tomatoes**,
  skinned (see page 11) and
  roughly chopped
4 tablespoons **water**
3 tablespoons chopped **fresh**
  coriander
2 tablespoons chopped **mint**
salt and **pepper**

Mix together the garlic, chilli, soy sauce, coriander and cumin seeds and vinegar in a small bowl and set aside.

Season the pork with salt and pepper.

Heat 2 tablespoons of the oil in a large frying pan and gently fry the potatoes, stirring frequently, for about 15 minutes until golden and tender. Lift out with a slotted spoon on to a plate.

Add another 2 tablespoons of the oil to the pan and fry the pork pieces, half at a time, for about 5 minutes, stirring frequently, until browned, lifting out with a slotted spoon on to the plate. Heat the remaining oil in the pan and gently fry the onions for about 10 minutes until softened and browned. Add the tomatoes, garlic mixture and measurement water and mix well.

Return the pork and potatoes to the pan and cook gently for 10 minutes until the pork is cooked through and tender and the tomatoes are pulpy. Stir in the chopped coriander and mint and check the seasoning, adding a little salt and pepper if necessary.

For crispy-cooked kale, to serve as an accompaniment, wash 200 g (7 oz) shredded curly kale and pat dry with kitchen paper. Place in a bowl and drizzle with 1 tablespoon vegetable oil. Sprinkle with 1 teaspoon caster sugar and season with salt and pepper. Mix the ingredients together thoroughly. (This is best done with your hands.) Turn into an oiled roasting tin and cook in a preheated oven, 190°C (375°F), Gas Mark 5, for 10 minutes until crispy, turning the kale halfway through cooking.

beef goulash

Serves **8**
Preparation time **10 minutes**
Cooking time **2–2½ hours**

1.5 kg (3 lb) **braising steak**
4 tablespoons **olive oil**
2 **onions**, sliced
2 **red peppers**, cored,
  deseeded and diced
1 tablespoon **smoked paprika**
2 tablespoons chopped
  marjoram
1 teaspoon **caraway seeds**
1 litre (1¾ pints) **beef stock**
  (see below for homemade)
5 tablespoons **tomato purée**
salt and **pepper**
French bread, to serve

Cut the beef into large chunks. Heat the oil in a flameproof casserole and fry the beef in batches until browned on all sides, lifting out with a slotted spoon on to a plate.

Add the onions and red peppers to the casserole and cook gently for 10 minutes until softened. Stir in the paprika, marjoram and caraway seeds and cook, stirring, for 1 minute.

Return the beef to the casserole, add the stock, tomato purée and salt and pepper to taste and bring to the boil, stirring. Reduce the heat, cover and cook gently for 1½–2 hours. If the sauce needs thickening, uncover for the final 30 minutes. Serve with French bread.

For homemade beef stock, place 750 g (1½ lb) shin of beef, cut into chunks, in a large saucepan and add 2 chopped onions, 2–3 chopped carrots, 2 roughly chopped celery sticks, 1 bay leaf, 1 bouquet garni, 4–6 black peppercorns and 1.8 litres (3 pints) cold water. Slowly bring to the boil, then reduce the heat, cover with a well-fitting lid and simmer gently for 2 hours, skimming off any scum that rises to the surface. Strain through a fine sieve, discarding the solids, and leave to cool. Cover and store in the refrigerator for up to several days or freeze for up to 6 months. This makes about 1.5 litres (2½ pints).

braised lamb with flageolet beans

Serves **4**

Preparation time **25 minutes**,
plus overnight soaking

Cooking time **1½–1¾ hours**

250 g (8 oz) **dried flageolet
beans**

½ **boneless leg of lamb**
in one piece, about 800g
(1 lb 10 oz)

4 tablespoons **olive oil**

500 g (1 lb) **cherry tomatoes**,
halved

1 teaspoon **caster sugar**

2 **red onions**, chopped

8 **garlic cloves**, peeled and
left whole

450 ml (¾ pint) **lamb stock**
(see below for homemade)

1 tablespoon chopped
rosemary

3 tablespoons **sun-dried
tomato paste**

2 tablespoons **capers in
brine**, rinsed and drained

salt and **pepper**

Soak the beans in a bowl of cold water overnight. Drain
and transfer to a flameproof casserole. Cover with fresh
cold water, bring to the boil and cook for 15 minutes.
Drain and set aside. Discard any areas of excess fat
from the lamb and cut the meat into 8 large chunky
pieces. Season with salt and pepper and set aside.

Wipe out the casserole. Heat 3 tablespoons of the oil
and fry the lamb in two batches, until browned on all
sides, lifting out with a slotted spoon on to a plate. Add
the tomatoes and sugar to the casserole and fry, turning
in the oil, for 3 minutes. Slide out onto a plate and wipe
out the pan. Add the remaining oil and onions and fry
for 5 minutes. Tip in the beans, garlic, stock, rosemary
and tomato paste. Bring to the boil, then reduce the
heat, cover and cook for 45 minutes or until the beans
are tender. The water should be almost absorbed; if not,
uncover, increase the heat and reduce.

Stir in the capers and push the lamb down into the
beans. Re-cover and cook gently for 8–10 minutes so
the lamb is still pink in the centre. (For well-cooked,
allow an extra 15 minutes.) Stir in the tomatoes and
heat. Season to taste and leave to stand for 15 minutes.

For homemade lamb stock, heat 1 tablespoon olive
oil in a large saucepan and fry 500 g (1 lb) lamb
bones until browned all over. Drain off the fat and add
1 large chopped onion, 2 chopped carrots, 2 chopped
celery sticks, 2 bay leaves, several thyme sprigs and
1 teaspoon peppercorns. Cover with water and bring
to the boil. Reduce the heat and cook for 2½–3 hours.
Strain through a sieve and leave to cool. Cover and
store in the refrigerator for up to several days or freeze.

jamaican goat curry

Serves **4**

Preparation time **25 minutes**, plus marinating

Cooking time about **2½ hours**

50 g (2 oz) **fresh root ginger**, grated

1 **Scotch bonnet chilli**, deseeded and finely chopped

2 teaspoons **ground cumin**

2 teaspoons **ground coriander**

½ teaspoon **ground allspice**

½ teaspoon **ground turmeric**

750 g (1½ lb) **boneless shoulder of goat**, cut into small cubes

2 tablespoons **vegetable oil**

2 **onions**, chopped

3 **garlic cloves**, crushed

200 ml (7 fl oz) **lamb** or **chicken stock** (see pages 110 and 36 for homemade)

400 ml (14 fl oz) **can coconut milk**

4 **tomatoes**, skinned (see page 11) and roughly chopped

500 g (1 lb) **waxy potatoes**, cut into 1.5 cm (¾ inch) dice

salt and **pepper**

Mix together the ginger, chilli and ground spices. Place the goat in a non-metallic bowl, add the spice blend and mix together well. Cover loosely and leave to marinate in the refrigerator for several hours or overnight.

Heat the oil in a flameproof casserole and fry the goat in batches, until deep golden on all sides, lifting out with a slotted spoon on to a plate. Add the onions to the casserole and fry gently for 5 minutes.

Stir in the garlic, stock, coconut milk and tomatoes and bring to a simmer. Return the goat to the casserole, cover and cook in a preheated oven, 150°C (300°F), Gas Mark 2, for 1½ hours or until the goat is tender. Add the potatoes to the casserole and return to the oven for a further 30–40 minutes until tender. Season to taste and serve in bowls.

For Caribbean rice, to serve as an accompaniment, heat 2 tablespoons vegetable oil in a large saucepan with a tight-fitting lid and fry 1 small chopped onion for 5 minutes until soft. Add 2 crushed garlic cloves, 1 teaspoon chopped thyme and ¼ teaspoon ground allspice. Rinse and drain 300 g (10 oz) white long-grain rice. Add to the pan and cook, stirring, for 1 minute. Pour in a 400 ml (14 fl oz) can coconut milk and 250 ml (8 fl oz) vegetable or chicken stock. Bring to the boil, then reduce the heat to its lowest setting and add a Scotch bonnet chilli. Cover and cook gently, stirring once or twice, for about 12 minutes until the rice is just tender and the liquid has been absorbed. Stir in a 400 g (13 oz) can red kidney or borlotti beans or pigeon peas, rinsed and drained, and 2 finely chopped spring onions. Remove the chilli, heat through and season to taste.

beef & potato hash

Serves **4**
Preparation time **15 minutes**
Cooking time **50 minutes**

2 tablespoons **vegetable oil**
750 g (1½ lb) **minced beef**
1 **fennel bulb**, trimmed
   and chopped
2 **celery sticks**, chopped
2 teaspoons **cornflour**
450 ml (¾ pint) **beef
   stock** (see page 108 for
   homemade)
3 tablespoons **tomato purée**
700 g (1 lb 6 oz) **waxy
   potatoes**, cut into 1.5 cm
   (¾ inch) chunks
4 **star anise**, broken into
   pieces and crushed using a
   pestle and mortar
3 tablespoons **soy sauce**
1 tablespoon **light
   muscovado sugar**
15 g (½ oz) roughly chopped
   fresh coriander
salt and **pepper**

Heat 1 tablespoon of the vegetable oil in a large heavy-based frying pan and fry the minced beef for 10 minutes, breaking it up with a wooden spoon and stirring until browned and all the moisture has evaporated.

Push the meat to one side of the pan, add the remaining oil, fennel and celery and fry for 5 minutes until softened. Mix the cornflour with a little of the stock in a cup until smooth. Add to the pan with the remaining stock, tomato purée, potatoes and star anise.

Bring to a simmer, stirring, then reduce the heat and cover with a lid or foil. Cook gently for about 30 minutes until the potatoes are tender, stirring occasionally and adding a dash more water if the pan runs dry.

Stir in the soy sauce and sugar and cook for a further 5 minutes, uncovered if necessary to thicken the juices. Season to taste with salt and pepper and stir in the coriander before serving.

For watercress salad, to serve as an accompaniment, remove any tough stalks from 100 g (3½ oz) watercress. Peel ½ cucumber and cut in half lengthways. Scoop out the seeds and thinly slice the flesh. Add to the watercress in a salad bowl and sprinkle with ½ bunch of spring onions, finely chopped. Whisk 3 tablespoons groundnut or vegetable oil with 2 teaspoons rice vinegar, ½ teaspoon caster sugar and a little salt and pepper. Drizzle over the salad.

indian lamb curry

Serves **4**
Preparation time **15 minutes**
Cooking time **1¾ hours**

50 g (2 oz) **blanched almonds**, roughly chopped
40 g (1½ oz) **butter** or **ghee**
8 **cloves**
½ teaspoon **dried chilli flakes**
10 **cardamom pods**
1 tablespoon lightly crushed **cumin seeds**
1 tablespoon lightly crushed **coriander seeds**
50 g (2 oz) **fresh root ginger**, grated
½ teaspoon **ground turmeric**
2 **onions**, chopped
3 **garlic cloves**, roughly chopped
1 kg (2 lb) **boneless shoulder of lamb**, cut into small chunks
6 **tomatoes**, skinned (see page 11) and roughly chopped
100 ml (3½ fl oz) **natural yogurt**
salt and **pepper**
chopped coriander, to garnish

Heat a dry flameproof casserole, add the almonds and cook for 1 minute until toasted.

Melt the butter or ghee in the casserole and add the cloves, chilli flakes, cardamom, cumin, coriander, ginger and turmeric. Fry over a gentle heat for 3 minutes. Add the onions and fry for 5 minutes, stirring constantly, until they colour. Add the garlic for the last few minutes.

Transfer the contents of the casserole to a food processor, add 100 ml (3½ fl oz) cold water and process to a smooth paste, scraping down the mixture from the side of the bowl.

Return the paste to the casserole and stir in the lamb, tomatoes and 100 ml (3½ fl oz) cold water. Bring to a simmer, then reduce the heat to its lowest setting. Stir in the yogurt. Cook very gently, uncovered and stirring the mixture occasionally, for about 1½ hours or until the lamb is very tender and the juices thickened. Season and then garnish with coriander to serve.

For pilau rice, to serve as an accompaniment, rinse and drain 325 g (11 oz) basmati rice. Melt 25 g (1 oz) butter in a large saucepan with a tight-fitting lid and gently fry 2 finely chopped shallots with 1 teaspoon cardamom pods and 2 tablespoons black or yellow mustard seeds. When the seeds start to pop, stir in the rice and cook, stirring, for 1 minute. Add 500 ml (17 fl oz) vegetable or chicken stock and ¼ teaspoon ground turmeric. Bring to the boil, then reduce the heat to its lowest setting, cover and cook for 12–15 minutes until the rice is tender and the water has been absorbed. Fluff up the rice with a fork and season to taste before serving.

pork with maple-roasted roots

Serves **6**
Preparation time **30 minutes**
Cooking time about **5 hours**

5 g (¼ oz) **thyme leaves,** chopped
5 **garlic cloves,** crushed
½ teaspoon c**araway seeds**
1 teaspoon **celery salt**
2.5 kg (5½ lb) **boneless shoulder of pork joint,** skin scored
300 g (10 oz) **baby onions** or **shallots**
1.25 kg (2½ lb) **new potatoes,** scrubbed
500 g (1 lb) **parsnips,** cut into wedges
400 g (13 oz) **carrots,** cut into wedges
100 ml (3½ fl oz) **maple syrup**
150 ml (¼ pint) **dry white wine**
300 ml (½ pint) **beef** or **chicken stock** (see page 108 or 36 for homemade)
salt and **pepper**

Mix together the thyme, garlic, celery salt and pepper. Use a sharp knife to cut several deep slits through the pork skin into the meat. Pack the garlic mixture into the slits. Rub salt over the skin. Put the pork in a large roasting tin and roast in a preheated oven, 220°C (425°F), Gas Mark 7, for 30 minutes. Reduce the oven temperature to 140°C (275°F), Gas Mark 1, and roast for a further 2 hours. Put the onions or shallots in a heatproof bowl, cover with boiling water and leave to stand. Drain and rinse in cold water. Peel away the skins, leaving the onions or shallots whole. Add to the pan with the vegetables, turning in the fat. Return to the oven for 2 hours, turning occasionally.

Transfer the pork to a carving platter. Cover with foil and leave to rest in a warm place. Increase the oven temperature to 220°C (425°F), Gas Mark 7. Drain off the excess fat from the tin and brush the vegetables with the maple syrup. Return to the oven for 25–30 minutes, turning once, until golden. Lift out into a dish.

Skim off the fat in the tin, retaining the meaty juices. Add the wine and stock, bring to the boil on the hob and cook for about 5 minutes until slightly thickened. Serve the carved meat with the vegetables and gravy.

For apple & pear butter, to serve alongside, place 2 each peeled, cored and chopped apples and pears in a saucepan with 15 g (½ oz) caster sugar, 1 tablespoon water and a pinch of ground cloves. Cook, stirring, for 10–15 minutes until tender. Mash with a masher. Cook a little further, to thicken. Dot in 50 g (2 oz) unsalted butter a squeeze of lemon juice and stir until melted. Turn into a serving dish and leave to cool. Cover and chill.

beef rendang

Serves **4**
Preparation time **25 minutes**
Cooking time **3 hours**

2 **lemon grass stalks**
6 **kaffir lime leaves**
1 large **onion**, roughly
chopped
4 **garlic cloves**, crushed
40 g (1½ oz) piece of **fresh
root ginger**, peeled and
roughly chopped
1½ teaspoons **ground
coriander**
½ teaspoon dried **chilli flakes**
½ teaspoon **salt**
½ teaspoon **ground turmeric**
4 tablespoons **water**
2 tablespoons **vegetable oil**
875 g (1¾ lb) **shin of beef**,
cut into large chunks
400 ml (14 fl oz) **can
coconut milk**
1 tablespoon **palm sugar** or
light muscovado sugar
chopped parsley, to garnish

Discard the woody ends from the lemon grass and
chop. Place in a food processor with the lime leaves,
onion, garlic, ginger, coriander, chilli flakes, salt, turmeric
and measurement water. Process to a smooth paste,
scraping down the mixture from the side of the bowl.

Heat the oil in a flameproof casserole and fry the beef
in batches until browned on all sides, lifting out with a
slotted spoon on to a plate. Tip in the spice paste and
cook over a very gentle heat, stirring, for about 4–5
minutes or until most of the moisture has evaporated.
(Add a dash of water if the paste starts to catch.)

Stir the coconut milk and sugar into the casserole and
bring to a simmer. Return the beef to the pan, cover and
cook in a preheated oven, 150°C (300°F), Gas Mark 2,
for about 2½ hours or until the meat is very tender.

Remove the lid and return the casserole to the hob.
Cook, stirring, for about 8–10 minutes until the moisture
has evaporated and the sauce thickly coats the meat.
Sprinkle with the chopped parsley and serve.

For spiced jasmine rice, to serve as accompaniment,
rinse and drain 300 g (10 oz) jasmine or basmati rice.
Heat 2 tablespoons vegetable oil in a large saucepan
with a tight-fitting lid and fry 1 halved cinnamon stick,
10 crushed cardamom pods and 1 teaspoon crushed
coriander seeds for 1 minute. Add the rice and cook,
stirring, for 2 minutes. Pour in 500 ml (17 fl oz) water
and bring to the boil. Reduce the heat to its lowest
setting, cover and cook for 12–15 minutes until the rice
is tender and the water absorbed. Fluff up with a fork,
stir in 4 tablespoons chopped coriander and a little salt.

braised lamb shanks & tapenade

Serves **4**
Preparation time **15 minutes**
Cooking time **2¼ hours**

1 tablespoon **plain flour**
4 large **lamb shanks**
2 tablespoons **olive oil**
1 large **onion**, chopped
150 ml (¼ pint) **dry white wine**
300 ml (½ pint) **lamb** or **chicken stock** (see pages 110 and 36 for homemade)
finely grated rind of 1 **small orange**
150 g (5 oz) ready-made or homemade **black olive tapenade** (see below)
200 g (7 oz) **artichoke hearts** in oil, drained and sliced
salt and **pepper**
basil leaves, to garnish
ciabatta, to serve

Season the flour with salt and pepper on a plate. Coat the lamb shanks with the flour.

Heat the oil in a large flameproof casserole and fry the lamb shanks for 5 minutes until browned on all sides, draining to a plate. Add the onion to the casserole and fry for 5 minutes until softened.

Stir the wine and stock into the casserole and bring to a gentle simmer. Add the orange rind and return the lamb to the pan. Cover and cook in a preheated oven, 160°C (325°F), Gas Mark 3, for 1½ hours.

Spoon the tapenade around the lamb, stirring it into the cooking juices. Return the casserole to the oven for a further 30 minutes or until the lamb is very tender and can be pulled easily from the bone with a fork.

Transfer the casserole to the hob and cook gently, uncovered, to thicken the sauce if very thin. Season to taste with salt and pepper and scatter the artichokes around the shanks. Cook for 5 minutes to heat through. Scatter with basil leaves and serve with ciabatta.

For homemade tapenade, place 100 g (3½ oz) pitted black olives, 2 tablespoons rinsed and drained capers in brine, 2 chopped garlic cloves, 50 g (2 oz) chopped sun-dried tomatoes, 6 drained canned anchovy fillets and 15 g (½ oz) parsley in a food processor. Process until smooth, scraping down the mixture from the side of the bowl. Add 100 ml (3½ fl oz) olive oil and process again until smooth. Season with a little pepper and transfer to a bowl. Cover and refrigerate for up to a week.

chorizo & chickpea stew

Serves **4**
Preparation time **5 minutes**
Cooking time **25 minutes**

500 g (1 lb) **new potatoes**, scrubbed
1 teaspoon **olive oil**
2 **red onions**, chopped
2 **red peppers**, cored, deseeded and chopped
100 g (3½ oz) **chorizo sausage**, thinly sliced
500 g (1 lb) **plum tomatoes**, chopped, or 400 g (13 oz) **can chopped tomatoes**, drained
410 g (13½ oz) **can chickpeas**, rinsed and drained
2 tablespoons chopped **parsley**, to garnish
garlic bread, to serve

Cook the potatoes in a saucepan of boiling water for 12–15 minutes until tender. Drain and then slice. Meanwhile, heat the oil in a large frying pan and fry the onions and red peppers over a medium heat for 3–4 minutes. Add the chorizo and cook, turning frequently, for 2 minutes.

Stir the potato slices, tomatoes and chickpeas into the pan and bring to the boil. Reduce the heat and cook gently for 10 minutes.

Scatter over the parsley to garnish and serve with some hot garlic bread to mop up all the juices.

For sausage & mixed bean stew, cook the potatoes, then fry the onions and red peppers in the oil as above. Add 4 pork sausages instead of the chorizo to the pan and cook for 4–5 minutes until browned on all sides. Lift the sausages from the pan and cut each into 6 thick slices. Return to the pan and add the potato slices and tomatoes as above but replace the chickpeas with a 400 g (13 oz) can mixed beans, rinsed and drained. Bring to the boil and cook as above. If you prefer a slightly hotter stew, add 1 deseeded and chopped red chilli when frying the onions and peppers.

pot-roasted lamb with figs

Serves **6**
Preparation time **30 minutes**, plus resting
Cooking time **2¼ hours**

75 g (3 oz) **pistachio nuts**, chopped and toasted
100 g (3½ oz) **dried figs**, chopped
¼ teaspoon **ground cloves**
3 tablespoons **chopped mint**
1 teaspoon **rosewater**
1.5 kg (3 lb) **boneless rolled shoulder of lamb joint**
2 tablespoons **clear honey**
200 ml (7 fl oz) **dry white wine**
750 g (1½ lb) **baby potatoes**, scrubbed
3 tablespoons **olive oil**
500 g (1 lb) **small courgettes**, cut into thick slices
salt and **pepper**

Mix together the pistachio nuts, figs, cloves, mint, rosewater and a little salt and pepper in a bowl.

Unroll the lamb, removing the string, and pack the stuffing down the centre and into the cavities and folds of the lamb. Re-roll and secure with more string. Sit in a large roasting tin, fat-side up, and rub a little salt and pepper over the surface. Roast in a preheated oven, 220°C (425°F), Gas Mark 7, for 30 minutes.

Reduce the oven temperature to 180°C (350°F), Gas Mark 4. Brush the honey over the lamb, then pour the wine into the roasting tin. Brush the potatoes with the oil, then scatter into the tin. Season to taste with salt and pepper. Return to the oven for a further 1¼ hours.

Add the courgettes to the roasting tin, turning them in the juices, and return to the oven for a further 30 minutes. Leave to rest in a warm place for 20 minutes before carving the lamb.

For apricot, cinnamon & walnut stuffing, to use instead of the pistachio stuffing, heat 1 tablespoon vegetable oil in a frying pan and gently fry 1 chopped onion until softened. Tip into a bowl and add 75 g (3 oz) chopped walnuts, 100 g (3½ oz) chopped ready-to-eat dried apricots, the finely grated rind of 2 lemons and ½ teaspoon ground cinnamon. Mix well and finish the recipe as above.

chestnut, rice & pancetta soup

Serves **4**
Preparation time **10 minutes**
Cooking time **35 minutes**

50 g (2 oz) **butter**
150 g (5 oz) **pancetta**, diced
1 **onion,** finely chopped
200 g (7 oz) **pack cooked peeled chestnuts**
150 g (5 oz) **risotto rice**
500 ml (17 fl oz) **chicken stock** (see page 36 for homemade)
150 ml (¼ pint) **milk**
salt and **pepper**

Melt half the butter in a saucepan and cook the pancetta and onion over a medium heat for 10 minutes.

Cut the chestnuts in half and add to the pan with the rice and stock. Bring to the boil, then reduce the heat and cook gently for 20 minutes or until the rice is tender and most of the liquid has been absorbed.

Heat the milk in a small saucepan until tepid, then stir into the rice with the remaining butter. Season to taste with salt and pepper. Cover and leave to stand for about 5 minutes before serving.

For fennel, rice & pancetta soup with garlic & anchovies, cook the pancetta in 25 g (1 oz) butter as above with 1 large trimmed and thinly sliced fennel bulb instead of the onion. Then add the rice and stock to the pan, omitting the chestnuts, and cook as above until the rice is tender. Meanwhile, place 50 ml (2 fl oz) milk, 6 peeled whole garlic cloves and 150 g (5 oz) drained anchovy fillets from a can or jar in a small saucepan and cook gently for 15 minutes, without letting the milk come to the boil, until the anchovies have melted into the milk and the garlic is soft. Use the back of a fork to mash the garlic against the side of the pan, then add 75 g (3 oz) butter and 75 ml (3 fl oz) extra virgin olive oil and stir until the butter has melted. Stir this mixture into the soup in place of the milk, then season to taste with salt and pepper, cover and leave to stand for 5 minutes before serving.

sausage ragu with polenta crust

Serves **4**
Preparation time **15 minutes**
Cooking time **1 hour**

750 g (1½ lb) **pork sausages
with garlic or herbs**
4 tablespoons **olive oil**
2 **onions**, chopped
2 **garlic cloves**, crushed
1½ teaspoons **fennel seeds**
400 g (13 oz) **passata**
150 ml (¼ pint) **red wine**
4 tablespoons **sun-dried
tomato paste**
2 tablespoons chopped
oregano
500 g (1 lb) ready-made or
homemade **polenta**
(see below)
75 g (3 oz) **Parmesan
cheese**, freshly grated
50 g (2 oz) **mature Cheddar
cheese**, grated
salt and **pepper**

Split the skins of the sausages with a knife, peel away
and discard.

Heat the oil in a shallow flameproof casserole or
heavy-based frying pan and gently fry the onions for
10 minutes until softened and pale golden, adding the
garlic for the last couple of minutes. Add the sausages
and fennel seeds and cook for 10 minutes, breaking up
the sausages with a wooden spoon, until golden.

Stir in the passata, wine, tomato paste and oregano.
Bring to a simmer, then reduce the heat to its lowest
setting, cover and cook gently for 30 minutes until
the sauce is thick and pulpy. Season to taste with salt
and pepper.

Break up the polenta into small pieces and crumble
over the sausages. Sprinkle with the Parmesan and
Cheddar and cook under a preheated moderate grill
for about 5 minutes until the cheese is melting and the
polenta is heated through.

For homemade polenta, bring 900 ml (1½ pints)
water to the boil with 1 teaspoon salt in a saucepan.
Add 150 g (5 oz) polenta in a stream, whisking
constantly to avoid lumps forming. Once it starts to
thicken, use a wooden spoon to stir the polenta while it
cooks for about 5 minutes until very thick and beginning
to hold its shape. Line a baking sheet with baking
parchment and pour the polenta out on to it. Leave until
cold, then use as above.

pork shins 'osso bucco'

Serves 4–5
Preparation time **15 minutes**
Cooking time **2–2½ hours**

1 tablespoon **plain flour**
1 kg (2 lb) **shin of pork**,
   thickly sliced
3 tablespoons **olive oil**
2 **onions**, finely chopped
2 **carrots**, diced
2 **celery sticks**, thinly sliced
300 ml (½ pint) **dry white
   wine**
400 g (13 oz) **can plum
   tomatoes**
4 tablespoons **sun-dried
   tomato paste**
150 ml (¼ pint) **chicken stock**
   (see page 36 for homemade)
1 **garlic clove**, finely chopped
finely grated rind of 1 **lemon**
3 tablespoons chopped
   parsley
salt and **pepper**

Season the flour with salt and pepper on a plate.
Coat the pork with the flour.

Heat 2 tablespoons of the oil in a large flameproof
casserole and fry the pork in batches until browned
on both sides, lifting out with a slotted spoon on to a
plate. Add the remaining oil to the casserole and gently
fry the onions, carrots and celery for 10 minutes until
softened. Add any flour left over from coating and cook,
stirring, for 1 minute.

Blend in the wine and bring to the boil, stirring. Stir in
the tomatoes, tomato paste, stock and a little salt and
pepper. Return the pork to the casserole, cover and
cook in a preheated oven, 160°C (325°F), Gas Mark 3,
for 1½–2 hours until the meat is very tender.

Mix together the garlic, lemon rind and parsley and
sprinkle over the casserole and serve.

For risotto Milanese, to serve as an accompaniment,
melt 25 g (1 oz) butter in a large saucepan and gently
fry 1 finely chopped onion for 5 minutes until softened.
Add 275 g (9 oz) risotto rice and cook, stirring, for
2 minutes. Gradually add 1.2 litres (2 pints) hot chicken
stock to the pan, a ladleful at a time, cooking and
stirring until each ladleful has been absorbed before
adding the next. This should take 20–25 minutes, by
which time the rice should be tender but retaining a
little bite and the consistency creamy. You may not
need all the stock. Crumble in 1 teaspoon saffron
threads towards the end of cooking. Once cooked, beat
in another 25 g (1 oz) butter and 50 g (2 oz) freshly
grated Parmesan cheese.

treacle & mustard beans

Serves **6**
Preparation time **10 minutes**
Cooking time **1 hour 35 minutes**

1 **carrot**, diced
1 **celery stick**, chopped
1 **onion**, chopped
2 **garlic cloves**, crushed
2 x 400 g (13 oz) **cans soya beans**, drained
700 g (1 lb 6 oz) **jar passata**
75 g (3 oz) **smoked bacon rashers**, diced
2 tablespoons **black treacle**
2 teaspoons **Dijon mustard**
salt and **pepper**

Place all the ingredients in a flameproof casserole and bring slowly to the boil, stirring occasionally.

Cover and bake in a preheated oven, 160°C (325°F), Gas Mark 3, for 1 hour.

Remove the lid and bake for a further 30 minutes and serve.

For garlic-rubbed sourdough bread, to serve as an accompaniment, heat a ridged griddle pan or large dry frying pan until hot and cook 6 thick slices of sourdough bread for 2 minutes on each side until lightly charred. Rub each bread slice with the cut sides of 1–2 peeled and halved garlic cloves and drizzle with extra virgin olive oil.

fish &
seafood

crab & coconut chowder

Serves **4**
Preparation time **15 minutes**
Cooking time **50 minutes**

25 g (1 oz) **butter**
1 tablespoon **vegetable oil**
1 large **onion**, chopped
200 g (7 oz) **lean belly pork**,
    finely diced
2 **garlic cloves**, crushed
150 ml (¼ pint) **dry white
    wine**
200 g (7 oz) **can chopped
    tomatoes**
400 ml (14 fl oz) **can coconut
    milk**
1 teaspoon **medium curry
    paste**
350 g (12 oz) **waxy potatoes**,
    diced
300 g (10 oz) **white** and
    brown crabmeat
3 tablespoons **double cream**
salt and **pepper**

Melt the butter with the oil in a large saucepan and gently fry the onion and pork, stirring, for about 10 minutes until lightly browned. Stir in the garlic and fry for 1 minute. Lift the pork out with a slotted spoon on to a plate.

Add the wine to the pan, bring to the boil and boil for about 5 minutes, until slightly reduced.

Return the pork to the pan, add the tomatoes, coconut milk, curry paste and potatoes and heat until simmering. Reduce the heat to its lowest setting, cover and cook for 30 minutes.

Stir in the crabmeat and cream, heat through thoroughly, and season to taste with salt and pepper. Serve hot with crusty bread, if liked.

For smoked haddock & sweetcorn chowder, melt 25 g (1 oz) butter in a large saucepan and gently fry 1 chopped onion and 1 chopped celery stick. Stir in 2 teaspoons crushed coriander seeds, ¼ teaspoon ground turmeric, 600 ml (1 pint) milk and 450 ml (¾ pint) fish or chicken stock. Bring just to the boil, then reduce the heat to its lowest setting. Stir in 500 g (1 lb) diced waxy potatoes and 625 g (1¼ lb) diced skinless smoked haddock fillet. Cover and cook gently for 10 minutes, then stir in 200 g (7 oz) sweetcorn and cook for a further 10 minutes. Season to taste with pepper and serve.

braised pollack with lentils

Serves **4**
Preparation time **15 minutes**
Cooking time **50 minutes**

4 tablespoons **olive oil**
1 **onion**, finely chopped
4 **garlic cloves**, crushed
2 teaspoons finely chopped
   rosemary, savoury or **thyme**
400 g (13 oz) **can green
   lentils**
400 g (13 oz) **can chopped
   tomatoes**
2 teaspoons **caster sugar**
150 ml (¼ pint) **fish
   stock** (see page 178 for
   homemade)
625 g (1¼ lb) **skinless
   pollack fillets**
4 tablespoons chopped
   parsley
50 g (2 oz) **can anchovy
   fillets**, drained and chopped
salt and **pepper**
garlic mayonnaise, to serve

Heat 2 tablespoons of the oil in a flameproof casserole and gently fry the onion for 6–8 minutes until lightly browned. Add the garlic and herb and cook for about 2 minutes.

Drain the lentils and stir into the casserole with the tomatoes, sugar and stock. Bring to a simmer, then cover and cook in a preheated oven, 180°C (350°F), Gas Mark 4, for 10 minutes. Check over the fish for any stray bones and cut into 8 pieces. Season with salt and pepper.

Stir the parsley and anchovies into the casserole. Nestle the fish down into the lentils and drizzle the fish with the remaining oil. Re-cover and return to the oven for a further 25 minutes or until the fish is cooked through. Serve with spoonfuls of garlic mayonnaise.

For salsa verde sauce, to serve as an alternative accompaniment to the garlic mayonnaise, roughly chop 25 g (1 oz) parsley and 15 g (½ oz) basil and place in a food processor with 1 roughly chopped garlic clove, 15 g (½ oz) pitted green olives, 1 tablespoon rinsed and drained capers in brine and ½ teaspoon Dijon mustard. Process until finely chopped. Add 1 tablespoon lemon juice and 125 ml (4 fl oz) olive oil and process to make a thick sauce. Season to taste with salt and pepper, adding a dash more lemon juice, if liked, for extra tang.

mediterranean fish stew

Serves **4–6**
Preparation time **30 minutes**
Cooking time **45 minutes**

1 large handful of **live mussels**
800 g (1 lb 9 oz) mixed **skinless white fish fillets,** such as pollack, haddock, halibut, bream, gurnard or mullet
4 tablespoons **olive oil**
1 large **onion**, chopped
2 small **fennel bulbs**, trimmed and chopped
5 **garlic cloves**, crushed
3 pared strips of **orange rind**
2 x 400 g (13 oz) **cans chopped tomatoes**
2 teaspoons **caster sugar**
4 tablespoons **sun-dried tomato paste**
500 ml (17 fl oz) **fish stock** (see page 178 for homemade)
1 teaspoon **saffron threads**
250 g (9 oz) cleaned **squid tubes**, cut into rings
salt and **pepper**

Scrub the mussels. Scrape off any barnacles and pull away any beards. Discard those that are damaged or open and do not close when tapped firmly. Check over the fish for any stray bones and cut into chunky pieces. Season with salt and pepper.

Heat the oil in a large flameproof casserole and fry the onion for 5 minutes. Add the fennel and fry, stirring, for 10 minutes. Add the garlic and orange rind and fry for 2 minutes. Add the tomatoes, sugar, tomato paste and fish stock. Crumble in the saffron and bring the stew to a gentle simmer. Cook gently, uncovered, for 15 minutes.

Lower the thickest, chunkiest pieces of fish into the stew. Reduce the heat to its lowest setting and cook for 5 minutes. Add the thin pieces of fish and the squid to the stew. Scatter the mussels on top and cover with a lid or foil. Cook for a further 5 minutes or until the mussel shells have opened. Ladle into large bowls, discarding any mussel shells that remain closed.

For homemade rouille, to serve as an accompaniment, spear a fork into a small red pepper and hold it over the hob on its highest setting until the skin blisters and browns. Remove from the heat and, when cool, peel away the skin. Roughly chop the flesh, discarding the core and seeds. Place in a food processor or blender with 2 chopped garlic cloves, 1 deseeded and chopped hot red chilli, 1 egg yolk and a little salt. Process to a paste. Add 25 g (1 oz) fresh white breadcrumbs and blend again until smooth. With the machine running, gradually drizzle in 100 ml (3½ fl oz) olive oil in a thin stream. Season with salt and transfer to a serving dish. Cover and chill until ready. Serve spooned over the stew.

mackerel with sesame noodles

Serves **2**
Preparation time **10 minutes**
Cooking time **12 minutes**

2 large **mackerel fillets**, about
    125 g (4 oz) each
2 tablespoons **teriyaki sauce**
2 teaspoons **sesame oil**
1 tablespoon **sesame seeds**
½ bunch of **spring onions**,
    chopped
1 **garlic clove**, very thinly
    sliced
100 g (3½ oz) **French beans**,
    topped and tailed and
    diagonally sliced
400 ml (14 fl oz) **fish
    stock** (see page 178 for
    homemade)
150 g (5 oz) **pack medium
    straight-to-wok rice
    noodles**
1 teaspoon **caster sugar**
2 teaspoons **lime juice**

Cut the mackerel into pieces and mix with the teriyaki sauce in a bowl.

Warm the sesame oil in a saucepan and add the sesame seeds, spring onions, garlic and beans. Heat through gently for 2 minutes.

Add the stock and bring to a gentle simmer. Cover and cook for 5 minutes.

Stir the mackerel, noodles, sugar and lime juice into the pan and cook gently for 2 minutes until the mackerel is cooked and the broth is hot. Serve immediately.

For cheat's pad thai, mix ½ teaspoon cornflour with 1 tablespoon lime juice in a small bowl until smooth. Add a further 2 tablespoons lime juice, ½ teaspoon chilli powder, 2 tablespoons caster sugar and 2 tablespoons Thai fish sauce. Heat 1 tablespoon vegetable oil or stir-fry oil in a large frying pan or wok over a high heat and stir-fry 150 g (5 oz) raw peeled prawns until they have turned pink. Add ½ bunch of spring onions, chopped, 200 g (7 oz) bean sprouts, 50 g (2 oz) chopped salted peanuts and a 150 g (5 oz) pack straight-to-wok rice noodles. Drizzle with the lime juice mixture and heat through, stirring, for a couple of minutes. Serve scattered with extra chopped peanuts and a small handful of chopped fresh coriander.

creamy garlic mussels

Serves **4**
Preparation time **15 minutes**
Cooking time **10 minutes**

1.5 kg (3 lb) **live mussels**
15 g (½ oz) **butter**
1 **onion**, finely chopped
6 **garlic cloves**, finely chopped
100 ml (3½ fl oz) **white wine**
150 ml (¼ pint) **single cream**
1 large handful of **flat leaf parsley**, roughly chopped
salt and **pepper**
crusty bread, to serve

Scrub the mussels in cold water. Scrape off any barnacles and pull away the dark hairy beards. Discard any with damaged shells or open ones that do not close when tapped firmly with a knife.

Melt the butter in a large saucepan and gently fry the onion and garlic for 2–3 minutes until transparent and softened.

Increase the heat and tip the mussels into the pan with the wine. Cover and cook, shaking the pan frequently, for 4–5 minutes until all the shells have opened. Discard any that remain closed.

Pour in the cream and heat through briefly, stirring well. Add the parsley, season well with salt and pepper and serve immediately in large bowls, with crusty bread to mop up the juices.

For mussels in spicy tomato sauce, cook the onion and garlic as above in 1 tablespoon olive oil instead of the butter, together with 1 deseeded and finely chopped red chilli. Add 1 teaspoon paprika and cook, stirring, for 1 minute, then add a 400 g (13 oz) can chopped tomatoes. Season to taste with salt and pepper, cover and cook gently for 15 minutes. Meanwhile, scrub and debeard the mussels as above. Then stir the mussels into the tomato sauce and increase the heat. Cover and cook for 4–5 minutes until all the shells have opened. Discard any that remain closed. Add the parsley and serve as above.

spanish baked fish

Serves **4**
Preparation time **5 minutes**
Cooking time **25 minutes**

4 chunky **skinless hake, cod**
  or **haddock fillets**, about
  150 g (5 oz) each
5 tablespoons **extra virgin**
  olive oil
40 g (1½ oz) **pine nuts**
50 g (2 oz) **raisins**
3 **garlic cloves**, thinly sliced
300 g (10 oz) **spinach**,
  washed and drained
lemon or **lime wedges**, for
  squeezing over
salt and **pepper**
rustic bread, to serve

Season the fish with salt and pepper. Drizzle a little of the oil into a roasting tin. Add the fish, spacing the pieces slightly apart, and brush with the remaining oil. Scatter the pine nuts and raisins into the tin.

Bake in a preheated oven, 190°C (375°F), Gas Mark 5, for 20 minutes or until the fish is cooked through.

Scatter the garlic into the roasting tin. Pile the spinach on top of the fish, making sure all the water has been thoroughly drained off the spinach first. Season lightly with salt and pepper and return to the oven for a further 5 minutes until the spinach has wilted.

Pile the spinach on to warmed serving plates and lay the fish on top. Spoon the pine nuts, raisins, garlic and cooking juices over the fish. Serve with lemon or lime wedges to squeeze over the fish and warmed rustic bread.

For quince alioli, to serve as an accompaniment, put 3 tablespoons quince jelly in a bowl and beat with a small whisk to break the jelly up. Whisk in 1 crushed garlic clove, plenty of pepper and 2 teaspoons lemon or lime juice. Gradually whisk in 4 tablespoons olive oil, a little at a time, until the consistency becomes smooth and thick. Transfer to a small bowl, cover and chill until ready to serve.

pea, dill & smoked salmon soup

Serves **4**
Preparation time **10 minutes**
Cooking time **30 minutes**

25 g (1 oz) **butter**
1 large **onion**, chopped
1 litre (1¾ pints) **fish
 stock** (see page 178 for
 homemade)
500 g (1 lb) **skinless lightly
 smoked salmon**
625 g (1¼ lb) **fresh** or
 frozen peas
15 g (½ oz) **dill,** chopped, plus
 extra for scattering
3 tablespoons **crème fraîche,**
 plus extra for topping
salt and **pepper**

Melt the butter in a large saucepan and fry the onion for 5 minutes until softened. Add the stock and bring to a gentle simmer. Lower the fish into the pan and cook gently for 5 minutes until the fish has turned opaque. Lift the fish out with a slotted spoon on to a plate.

Add the peas to the saucepan and bring to the boil. Reduce the heat to its lowest setting, cover and cook for 15 minutes. Ladle about half the soup into a food processor or blender and process until smooth. Return to the pan.

Flake the salmon into small pieces and add to the pan with the dill and crème fraîche. Heat through gently and season to taste with salt and pepper.

Ladle the soup into serving bowls and spoon a little of the crème fraîche on top of each. Serve scattered with extra dill.

For creamed sweetcorn & cockle soup, fry the onion and add the stock as above. Add 450 g (14½ oz) frozen sweetcorn and 300 g (10 oz) diced waxy potatoes. Reduce the heat to a gentle simmer and cook, covered, for 15 minutes. Add 250 g (8 oz) cooked frozen cockles (not those preserved in vinegar), 5 g (¼ oz) tarragon leaves and 1 teaspoon mild curry paste. Cook gently for a further 5 minutes. Blend the soup using an immersion blender or in a food processor and stir in 3 tablespoons crème fraîche. Reheat gently, season to taste with salt and pepper and serve.

seafood casserole

Serves **4**
Preparation time **20 minutes**
Cooking time **15 minutes**

200 g (7 oz) **live mussels**
200 g (7 oz) **clams** (or extra
  mussels if unavailable)
3 tablespoons **olive oil**
2 **red onions**, finely diced
2 **garlic cloves**, crushed
½ teaspoon **dried chilli flakes**
200 g (7 oz) **cleaned baby
  squid**, cut into thin strips,
  tentacles reserved
300 g (10 oz) **raw shell-on
  king prawns**
150 ml (¼ pint) **hot fish
  stock** (see page 178 for
  homemade)
150 ml (¼ pint) **dry white
  wine**
½ teaspoon crumbled
  saffron threads
8 **tomatoes**, skinned (see
  page 11) and deseeded
1 **bay leaf**
1 teaspoon **caster sugar**
400 g (13 oz) **red mullet** or
  sea bass fillets, cut into
  bite-sized pieces
salt and **pepper**

Scrub the mussels and clams in cold water. Scrape off any barnacles from the mussels and pull away the dark hairy beards. Discard any mussels or clams with damaged shells or open ones that do not close when tapped firmly with a knife. Set aside.

Heat the oil in a large saucepan and gently fry the onions and garlic for 5 minutes. Stir in the chilli flakes, then add the mussels and clams with the squid and king prawns and stir well.

Stir in the hot stock, wine, saffron, tomatoes, bay leaf and sugar and season with salt and pepper. Cover and cook for 5 minutes. Discard any mussels or clams that remain closed.

Add the fish, re-cover and cook gently for 5 minutes until cooked through. Serve immediately.

For creamy seafood hot pot, replace the red onions with 2 white onions and cook with the garlic as above, adding 1 bunch of spring onions, sliced, with the chilli flakes. Add the seafood as above, stir in the stock, wine, saffron, bay leaf and sugar, omitting the tomatoes, and bring to the boil. Season to taste with salt and pepper and cook, uncovered, for about 5 minutes until the wine has reduced by half. Stir in 200 ml (7 fl oz) crème fraîche and 300 ml (½ pint) double cream and cook for a further 5 minutes. Mix 1 tablespoon cornflour with 2 tablespoons cold water in a cup until smooth and add to the casserole with 2 tablespoons chopped parsley and the finely grated rind of 1 lemon. Cook, stirring, until slightly thickened. Serve with rice and a simple salad.

smoked fish pie

Serves **4**

Preparation time **35 minutes**, plus chilling

Cooking time **1 hour**

625 g (1¼ lb) **skinless smoked haddock, pollack** or **cod fillets**

1 teaspoon **cornflour**

4 **eggs**, soft-boiled shelled

1 **bunch of spring onions**, chopped

1 tablespoon **green peppercorns in brine**, rinsed and drained

15 g (½ oz) **parsley**, chopped

150 g (5 oz) **fresh peas**

500 ml (17 fl oz) ready-made or homemade **cheese sauce** (see below)

Potato pastry

200 g (7 oz) **floury potatoes**

250 g (8 oz) **plain flour**, plus extra for dusting

½ teaspoon **sea salt flakes**, plus extra for sprinkling

75 g (3 oz) **firm butter**, cut into small pieces

50 g (2 oz) **firm lard**, diced

1 teaspoon **Dijon mustard**

beaten egg, to glaze

Make the potato pastry. Finely grate the potatoes, then pat dry between several layers of kitchen paper. Place the flour in a bowl, add the salt, butter and lard and rub in with the fingertips until the mixture resembles coarse breadcrumbs. Mix in the potatoes. Mix the mustard with 1 tablespoon cold water in a cup, add to the bowl and mix to a firm dough with a round-bladed knife, adding a dash more water if the dough feels dry and crumbly. Wrap and chill for at least 30 minutes.

Check over the fish for any stray bones, then cut into small chunks. Toss with the cornflour in a small bowl and scatter into a shallow ovenproof dish or pie dish. Push the eggs down between the pieces of fish.

Scatter the spring onions, peppercorns, parsley and peas into the dish and spoon the sauce on top. Roll out the pastry on a lightly floured surface until slightly larger than the dish. Brush the rim of the dish with water and lay the pastry over, trimming off the excess. Crimp the pastry edges and make a hole in the centre. Brush with beaten egg and sprinkle with salt. Bake in a preheated oven, 200°C (400°F), Gas Mark 6, for 20 minutes. Reduce the temperature to 160°C (325°F), Gas Mark 3, and cook for 40 minutes until the pastry is deep golden.

For homemade Parmesan cheese sauce, melt 40 g (1½ oz) butter in a saucepan, add 40 g (1½ oz) plain flour and mix well over a medium heat for 1 minute, making a paste. Remove from the heat and blend 375 ml (13 fl oz) milk into the paste. Return to the heat and cook, stirring, until the sauce is thick and bubbling. Beat in 75 g (3 oz) grated Parmesan and season to taste. Transfer to a bowl and leave to cool.

154

stuffed bream with samphire

Serves **4**
Preparation time **20 minutes**
Cooking time **55 minutes**

750 g (1 ½ lb) **Maris Piper
potatoes**, thinly sliced
6 tablespoons **olive oil**
1 tablespoon chopped **thyme**
4 **bream fillets**, about 150 g
(5 oz) each
75 g (3 oz) **prosciutto**,
chopped
2 **shallots**, finely chopped
finely grated rind of 1 **lemon**
200 g (7 oz) **samphire**
salt and **pepper**

Toss the potato slices with 4 tablespoons of the oil, a little salt and pepper and the thyme in a bowl. Tip into a roasting tin or ovenproof dish and spread out in an even layer. Cover with foil and bake in a preheated oven, 190°C (375°F), Gas Mark 5, for about 30 minutes until the potatoes are tender.

Score the bream fillets with a sharp knife. Mix the prosciutto with the shallots, lemon rind and a little pepper and use to sandwich the bream fillets together. Tie at intervals with string. Cut each of the sandwiched fillets through the centre to make 4 even-sized portions.

Lay the fish over the potatoes and return to the oven, uncovered, for a further 20 minutes or until the fish is cooked through.

Scatter the samphire around the fish and drizzle with the remaining oil. Return to the oven for a further 5 minutes before serving.

For bacon-wrapped trout with potatoes, bake the potatoes as above. Score 4 whole descaled and gutted trout along each side and tuck several herb sprigs, such as parsley, tarragon or dill, into the cavity of each fish. Wrap 2 smoked streaky bacon rashers around each fish and lay over the potato base. Bake, uncovered, in the oven for a further 25–30 minutes until the bacon is crisp and the fish is cooked through.

halibut with roasted vegetables

Serves **4**
Preparation time **25 minutes**
Cooking time **about 1 hour**

250 g (9 oz) **shallots**
625 g (1¼ lb) **small whole
beetroot**, scrubbed and cut
into wedges
625 g (1¼ lb) **baby potatoes**,
scrubbed
1 small **fennel bulb**, trimmed
and cut into wedges
7 tablespoons **olive oil**
plenty of **rosemary sprigs**
8 **garlic cloves**, peeled
4 **halibut steaks**, about
150–175 g (5–6 oz) each
6 **canned anchovy fillets**,
drained
1 tablespoon **lemon juice**
2 tablespoons chopped
parsley
salt and **pepper**

Place the shallots in a heatproof bowl, cover with boiling water and leave to stand for 2 minutes. Drain and rinse in cold water. Peel away the skins, leaving the shallots whole.

Scatter the shallots in a roasting tin with the beetroot, potatoes and fennel. Drizzle with 3 tablespoons of the olive oil and roast in a preheated oven, 220°C (425°F), Gas Mark 7, for 45–50 minutes or until the vegetables are lightly roasted. Add the rosemary sprigs and garlic after half an hour of cooking.

Season the halibut steaks on both sides and lay over the vegetables. Return the roasting tin to the oven for a further 15 minutes or until the fish is cooked through.

Chop the anchovy fillets finely and whisk with the remaining olive oil, lemon juice, parsley and a little salt and pepper in a bowl to make a dressing.

Pile the halibut and vegetables on to warmed serving plates and spoon the dressing over the fish to serve.

For baked cod with anchovies & tomatoes, heat 2 tablespoons olive oil in a roasting tin on the hob and fry 1 small chopped red onion for 5 minutes until softened. Add 2 teaspoons finely chopped rosemary, 6 drained and finely chopped canned anchovy fillets, 12 pitted black olives and 500 g (1 lb) quartered tomatoes. Mix well. Season 4 chunky skinless cod fillets, about 175 g (6 oz) each, and push down into the centre of the tin. Drizzle with a little extra olive oil and bake in a preheated oven, 190°C (375°F), Gas Mark 5, for about 25 minutes until the fish is cooked through.

baked sardines with mozzarella

Serves **2**
Preparation time **10 minutes**
Cooking time **30 minutes**

1 **small onion**, finely chopped
2 **garlic cloves**, thinly sliced
1 **celery stick**, thinly sliced
3 tablespoons **extra virgin
olive oil**
100 g (3½ oz) **piquillo
peppers** from a jar or
can, drained
1 tablespoon **capers in brine**,
rinsed and drained
4 **large filleted sardines**
100 g (3½ oz) **mozzarella
cheese balls**
4 slices of **ciabatta**
salt and **pepper**

Place the onion, garlic and celery in a small roasting tin
or ovenproof dish with 1 tablespoon of the oil. Mix well.
Cook in a preheated oven, 200°C (400°F), Gas Mark 6,
for 10 minutes until softened.

Slice the peppers thinly and add to the roasting tin
with the capers and season lightly with salt and pepper.
Lay the sardines on top and drizzle with another
tablespoon of the oil. Return the roasting tin to the
oven for a further 15 minutes until the sardines are
cooked through.

Add the mozzarella to the roasting tin and return to the
oven for a final 2 minutes.

Toast the ciabatta for 1–2 minutes on both sides.

Arrange the toasted ciabatta on warmed serving plates
and pile the sardines and vegetables on top. Serve
drizzled with the pan juices and the remaining oil.

For baked tuna with chargrilled vegetables, cook
the onion, garlic and celery as above. Add 2 tuna steaks,
about 125 g (4 oz) each, and 150 g (5 oz) sliced ready-
prepared chargrilled red peppers to the roasting tin and
return to the oven for 10 minutes. Add 8 black olives
and a squeeze of lemon to the tin and return to the oven
for a further 2 minutes. Flake the tuna into pieces and
pile on to toasted ciabatta with the vegetables as above,
drizzling with another 1 tablespoon extra virgin olive oil.

baked prawns & fruit couscous

Serves **2**
Preparation time **20 minutes**
Cooking time **40 minutes**

200 g (7 oz) **raw peeled prawns**
1 large **onion**, chopped
1 **medium-strength green chilli,** deseeded and finely chopped
2 **garlic cloves**, thinly sliced
1 teaspoon **fennel seeds**
½ teaspoon **smoked paprika**
4 tablespoons **olive oil**
150 g (5 oz) **couscous**
200 ml (7 fl oz) **hot fish** or **chicken stock** (see pages 178 and 36 for homemade)
15 g (½ oz) **fresh coriander**, chopped
175 g (6 oz) **ready-prepared chargrilled artichokes**, sliced
2 **ripe peaches** or **nectarines**, stoned and sliced
salt and **pepper**

Pat the prawns dry between several layers of kitchen paper.

Place the onion, chilli, garlic, fennel seeds, paprika and oil in a shallow casserole and mix well. Cover and cook in a preheated oven, 180°C (350°F), Gas Mark 4, for 20 minutes until the onions are soft.

Add the prawns and return the casserole to the oven, uncovered, for a further 15 minutes or until the prawns have turned pink.

Meanwhile, place the couscous in a heatproof bowl and add the hot stock. Leave to stand for 5 minutes until the stock has been absorbed.

Fluff the couscous up with a fork and add to the casserole with the coriander, artichokes and peaches or nectarines. Mix well and season to taste with salt and pepper. Re-cover and return to the oven for a final 5 minutes to heat through.

For pesto prawns with couscous, place 50 g (2 oz) pine nuts in a shallow casserole and toast in a preheated oven, 180°C (350°F), Gas Mark 4, for about 8–10 minutes. Tip the pine nuts out into a bowl. Cook the onion, garlic and oil and then the prawns in the casserole as above, omitting the chilli, fennel seeds and paprika. Prepare the couscous with the stock as above and add to the casserole with 5 tablespoons ready-made green pesto, 2 stoned and sliced ripe peaches, 15 g (½ oz) torn basil leaves and the toasted pine nuts. Mix well and season to taste with salt and pepper. Return to the oven for a final 5 minutes to heat through.

smoked clam & bacon gratin

Serves **4**
Preparation time **25 minutes**
Cooking time about **1½ hours**

750 g (1½ lb) **small waxy potatoes**
2 x 150 g (5 oz) **cans smoked clams**, drained
75 g (3 oz) **lean back bacon rashers**, finely diced
3 **shallots**, thinly sliced
250 ml (8 fl oz) **single cream**
250 ml (8 fl oz) **milk**
1 tablespoon chopped **thyme**
2 **garlic cloves**, crushed
50 g (2 oz) **Gruyère cheese**, finely grated
50 g (2 oz) **fresh white breadcrumbs**
40 g (1½ oz) **butter**, melted, plus extra for greasing
pepper

Grease a 2 litre (3½ pint) shallow ovenproof dish. Scrub and thinly slice the potatoes, then layer half into the dish.

Chop the clams roughly and scatter over the potatoes with the bacon and shallots. Arrange the remaining potato slices on top.

Beat together the cream, milk, thyme, garlic and half the Gruyère in a bowl. Season with plenty of pepper and pour over the potatoes. Cover with foil and bake in a preheated oven, 180°C (350°F), Gas Mark 4, for 45 minutes.

Stir the breadcrumbs into the melted butter until coated. Scatter over the potatoes and sprinkle with the remaining Gruyère. Return to the oven, uncovered, for a further 45–50 minutes until the potatoes are tender and the topping is golden. Serve with a green or tomato salad, if liked.

For roast tomatoes with capers, to serve as an accompaniment, halve 750 g (1½ lb) small ripe tomatoes and place, cut-side up, in a roasting tin. Sprinkle with ½ teaspoon caster sugar, a little salt and pepper and 1 teaspoon dried oregano. Drizzle with 3 tablespoons olive oil and scatter with 2 tablespoons rinsed and drained capers in brine. Bake in a preheated oven, 180°C (350°F), Gas Mark 4, for 50–60 minutes until the tomatoes are tender and lightly coloured.

classic paella

Preparation time **40 minutes**
Cooking time about **1½ hours**
Serves **6**

1 kg (2 lb) **live mussels**
4 **garlic cloves**
1 small bunch of **mixed herbs**
150 ml (¼ pint) **dry**
  white wine
2 litres (3½ pints) **hot chicken**
  stock (see page 36 for
  homemade) or **water**
4 tablespoons **olive oil**
4 **small cleaned squid**, cut
  into rings
1 large **onion**, finely chopped
1 **red pepper**, cored,
  deseeded and chopped
4 large **ripe tomatoes**,
  skinned (see page 11),
  deseeded and chopped
12 **skinless, boneless**
  chicken thighs, cut into
  bite-sized pieces
500 g (1 lb) **paella rice**
large pinch of **saffron threads**,
  crumbled
125 g (4 oz) **fresh** or **frozen**
  peas
12 large **raw peeled prawns**
salt and **pepper**

Scrub the mussels in cold water. Scrape off any barnacles and pull away the dark hairy beads. Discard any with damaged shells or open ones that do not close when tapped firmly with a knife. Set aside.

Slice 2 of the garlic cloves and crush the remainder. Place the sliced garlic in a large heavy-based saucepan with the herbs, wine and 150 ml (¼ pint) of the hot stock or water and season well with salt and pepper. Tip in the mussels, cover and cook, shaking the pan frequently, for 4–5 minutes until all the shells have opened. Lift out with a slotted spoon into a bowl, discarding any that remain closed. Strain the cooking liquid and reserve.

Heat 2 tablespoons of the oil in the pan and fry the squid, stirring frequently, for 5 minutes. Add the onion, red pepper and crushed garlic and cook gently for 5 minutes until softened. Add the mussel cooking liquid and tomatoes and season with salt and pepper. Bring to the boil, then reduce the heat and cook gently, stirring, for 15–20 minutes until thickened. Transfer to a bowl.

Fry the chicken in the remaining oil in the pan for 5 minutes. Add the rice and cook, stirring, for 3 minutes. Return the squid mixture, add one-third of the remaining stock and the saffron and bring to the boil, stirring. Cover and simmer, adding stock a little at a time, for 30 minutes or until the chicken is cooked, the rice is tender and the liquid has been absorbed. Check the seasoning, add the peas and prawns and simmer, for 5 minutes, adding a little more stock if required. Add the mussels, cover and heat through for 5 minutes. Serve immediately.

cod with oven chips & mint peas

Serves **4**
Preparation time **20 minutes**
Cooking time **1 hour 10 minutes**

1 kg (2 lb) **baking potatoes**
5 tablespoons **vegetable oil**
good pinch each of **ground paprika, celery salt** and **ground cumin**
4 **chunky cod fillets**, about 150–175 g (5–6 oz) each
20 g (¾ oz) **butter**
400 g (13 oz) **fresh** or **frozen peas**
100ml (3½ fl oz) **fish** or **chicken stock** (see pages 178 and 36 for homemade)
1 tablespoon chopped **mint**
2 tablespoons **crème fraîche**
salt and **pepper**

Scrub the potatoes and cut into 1 cm (½ inch) thick slices. Cut across into chunky chips. Place in a bowl and drizzle with the oil, then turn in the oil until coated. Sprinkle with the paprika, celery salt and cumin and mix.

Heat a large roasting tin in a preheated oven, 200°C (400°F), Gas Mark 6, for 3 minutes. Tip in the potatoes and spread out in an even layer. Bake in the oven for about 40 minutes, turning the potatoes a couple of times, until evenly pale golden.

Season the pieces of fish with salt and pepper. Slide the potatoes to one side of the roasting tin and add the fish. Dot with the butter and return the roasting tin to the oven for a further 20 minutes or until the fish is cooked through. Transfer the fish and chips to warmed serving plates and return to the oven, with the door left open, to keep warm.

Add the peas and stock to the roasting tin and bring to the boil on the hob. Boil for 3 minutes or until the peas are tender. Tip the contents of the roasting tin into a food processor, add the mint and crème fraîche and process to a purée. Serve with the fish and chips.

For homemade tomato ketchup, to serve as an accompaniment, roughly chop 625 g (1¼ lb) ripe tomatoes and place in a saucepan with 1 roughly chopped onion, 50 g (2 oz) light muscovado sugar, ¼ teaspoon cayenne pepper, ½ teaspoon salt and 50 ml (2 fl oz) red wine vinegar. Bring to the boil, then reduce the heat and cook very gently, stirring frequently, for about 30 minutes until the sauce is thickened. Press through a sieve into a bowl. Leave to cool, then serve.

squid with black rice

Serves **4**
Preparation time **20 minutes**
Cooking time **35 minutes**

500 g (1 lb) **cleaned
    squid tubes**
4 tablespoons **olive oil**
1 **onion**, finely chopped
3 **garlic cloves**, crushed
300 g (10 oz) **paella rice**
15 g (½ oz) **squid ink**
900ml (1½ pints) **fish** or
    chicken stock (see pages
    178 and 36 for homemade)
2 teaspoons chopped **thyme**
150 ml (¼ pint) **dry
    white wine**
15 g (½ oz) **parsley**,
    finely chopped
lime wedges, for squeezing
    over, to serve
salt and **pepper**

Cut the squid into 5 mm (¼ inch) thick rings. Pat dry between several layers of kitchen paper. Heat the oil in a large saucepan and gently fry the squid rings, half at a time, until they have turned opaque. Lift out on to a plate. Add the onion to the pan and fry for 5 minutes until softened, adding the garlic for the last couple of minutes. Stir in the rice and cook for 2 minutes until coated in the oil and juices. Blend the squid ink with 2 tablespoons of the stock and set aside.

Stir the thyme and wine into the pan and cook quickly, stirring, until the wine has been absorbed. Pour in the remaining stock and bring to the boil. Reduce the heat to its lowest setting and cook, uncovered and stirring frequently, for about 20 minutes until the rice is tender and the stock absorbed. Add more stock if too dry.

Return the squid to the pan and add the squid ink mixture and half the parsley. Stir well and season to taste with salt and pepper. Ladle into bowls and sprinkle with remaining parsley. Serve with lime wedges.

For red rice, saffron & seafood pilaf, melt 40 g (1½ oz) butter in a frying pan and fry 1 large finely chopped onion, 2 chopped celery sticks and 50 g (2 oz) toasted flaked almonds for 5 minutes. Rinse and drain 250 g (8 oz) red rice. Add to the pan with 500 ml (17 fl oz) stock, the grated rind of ½ orange, ½ teaspoon ground cumin and ½ teaspoon crumbled saffron threads. Bring to a simmer and cook, stirring, for 35–40 minutes until tender. Add more stock if needed. Cut 400 g (13 oz) monkfish or other firm-textured skinless white fish fillets into pieces and stir in the rice with chopped coriander. Cook for a few minutes. Serve.

butter bean & chilli prawn soup

Serves **4**
Preparation time **15 minutes**,
  plus overnight soaking
Cooking time **50 minutes**

250 g (8 oz) **dried butter beans**
500 g (1 lb) **raw peeled prawns**
½ teaspoon **hot chilli powder**
2 tablespoons **olive oil**
4 tablespoons **sun-dried tomato paste**
2 teaspoons **caster sugar**
100 g (3½ oz) **streaky bacon rashers**, finely chopped
2 **onions**, roughly chopped
3 **bay leaves**
salt
roughly chopped **parsley**,
  to garnish

Soak the beans in a bowl of cold water overnight and then drain.

Pat the prawns dry between several layers of kitchen paper. Dust lightly with the chilli powder and a little salt.

Heat the oil in a large saucepan and fry the prawns briefly on both sides until they have turned pink. Stir in the tomato paste, sugar and 2 tablespoons water. Cook over a gentle heat, stirring, for 1 minute, then scrape out on to a plate.

Add the bacon to the pan and cook until browned. Stir in the drained beans, onions, bay leaves and 1 litre (1¾ pints) cold water and bring to a gentle simmer. Reduce the heat, cover and cook very gently for 40 minutes or until the beans are soft.

Remove the bay leaves. Blend the soup using an immersion blender or in a food processor. Return to the pan and reheat gently, stir in half the prawns and season to taste with salt and pepper.

Ladle the soup into serving bowls and spoon the remaining prawns and their cooking juices on top. Serve garnished with roughly chopped parsley.

For simple prawn & pesto pasta, bring a large saucepan of salted water to the boil. Add 300 g (10 oz) dried tagliatelle and cook for 10 minutes or until the pasta is just tender. Drain lightly and return to the pan. Add 400 g (13 oz) cooked peeled prawns, a 200 g (7 oz) jar sun-dried tomato pesto, 4 tablespoons crème fraîche and salt and pepper to taste. Heat through gently for 2 minutes before serving.

mussel & potato hotpot

Serves **2**
Preparation time **15 minutes**
Cooking time **30 minutes**

1 kg (2 lb) **live mussels**
25 g (1 oz) **butter**
1 **onion**, chopped
3 **garlic cloves**, crushed
150 ml (¼ pint) **dry white wine**
500 g (1 lb) **baby potatoes**, scrubbed
50 g (2 oz) **curly parsley**, roughly chopped
150 ml (¼ pint) **single cream**
salt and **pepper**

Prepare the mussels as described in the first step on page 142. Melt the butter in a large saucepan and gently fry the onion for 5 minutes until softened, adding the garlic for the last couple of minutes. Pour in the wine and bring to the boil. Tip the mussels into the pan, cover and cook, shaking the pan often, for 4–5 minutes until all the shells are open. Lift out with a slotted spoon into a bowl.

Add the potatoes to the cooking juices in the pan, re-cover and cook gently for 15 minutes or until the potatoes are cooked through, adding a little water if the pan runs dry. Meanwhile, remove about two-thirds of the mussels from their shells, discarding any closed shells.

Place the parsley and cream in a food processor and process until the parsley is finely chopped. Pour into the pan. Bring to the boil and boil briefly until the juices have thickened slightly. Return all the mussels to the pan and heat through gently for a couple of minutes. Season with pepper and a little salt and serve in bowls.

For easy herb soda bread, to serve alongside, mix 250 g (8 oz) plain flour, 250 g (8 oz) wholemeal flour, 1 teaspoon bicarbonate of soda and 1½ teaspoons salt in a bowl. Add 50 g (2 oz) butter, cubed, and rub in with fingertips until the mixture is like breadcrumbs. Add 50g (2 oz) chopped herbs and 275 ml (9 fl oz) buttermilk and mix to a dough with a round-bladed knife. Tip out on a lightly floured surface, shape into a ball and place on a greased baking sheet. Slash the top first in one direction and then the other. Bake in a preheated oven, 220°C (425°F), Gas Mark 7, for 30 minutes or until golden and the base sounds hollow when tapped.

keralan seafood curry

Serves **4**
Preparation time **20 minutes**
Cooking time **35 minutes**

750 g (1½ lb) **chunky
skinless white fish fillets**,
such as cod or pollack
3 tablespoons **vegetable oil**
1 tablespoon **yellow
mustard seeds**
½ teaspoon **fenugreek seeds**
1 teaspoon **ground coriander**
1 **medium-strength green
chilli**, deseeded and finely
chopped
1 small **onion**, thinly sliced
3 **garlic cloves**, crushed
50 g (2 oz) piece of **fresh root
ginger**, grated
½ teaspoon **ground turmeric**
400 ml (14 fl oz) **can coconut
milk**
200 g (7 oz) **can chopped
tomatoes**
200 g (7 oz) **cleaned squid
tubes**, cut into thin rings
salt

Check over the fish for any stray bones, then cut into chunky pieces.

Heat 2 tablespoons of the oil in a large flameproof casserole or saucepan and gently cook the mustard and fenugreek seeds until they start to pop. Add the coriander, chilli and onion and cook very gently, stirring, for 5 minutes.

Stir the garlic, ginger and turmeric into the pan, then spoon the ingredients out on to a plate. Add the remaining oil to the pan and fry the fish for 3–4 minutes, until coloured on all sides, turning the pieces gently. Lift out with a slotted spoon on to a separate plate.

Return the spice mixture to the pan and add the coconut milk. Bring to a gentle simmer, cover and cook for 10 minutes.

Stir in the tomatoes and return the fish to the pan with the squid. Cover and cook gently for a further 10 minutes before serving in shallow bowls.

For Keralan perfumed rice to serve alongside, rinse and drain 300 g (10 oz) basmati rice. Melt 25 g (1 oz) butter or ghee in a saucepan and gently cook 1 teaspoon cardamom pods, 1 halved cinnamon stick, several crumbled curry leaves and 1 finely chopped shallot, stirring, for 3 minutes. Add the rice and cook, stirring, for 2 minutes. Pour in 500 ml (17 fl oz) water and bring to the boil. Reduce the heat to its lowest setting, cover and cook for 12–15 minutes until the rice is tender and the water has been absorbed. Fluff up the rice with a fork and season to taste with salt and pepper to serve.

salt cod minestrone

Serves **4**
Preparation time **20 minutes**,
  plus **1–2 days' soaking**
Cooking time **50 minutes**

500 g (1 lb) **salt cod**
4 tablespoons **olive oil**
2 **onions**, chopped
1 small **aubergine**, diced
3 **garlic cloves**, crushed
1.2 litres (2 pints) **fish stock**
  (see below for homemade)
2 tablespoons chopped
  oregano
2 tablespoons **tomato purée**
100 g (3½ oz) **dried**
  spaghetti, snapped into
  short lengths
400 g (13 oz) **cherry**
  tomatoes, quartered
6–8 large **green cabbage**
  leaves or **cavolo nero**,
  finely shredded

Soak the salt cod in a bowl of cold water for 1–2 days, changing the water several times. Drain the cod and cut into small chunks, discarding any skin and bones.

Heat 2 tablespoons of the oil in a large saucepan and fry the onions and aubergine very gently, stirring frequently, for about 10 minutes until lightly browned, adding the garlic for the last couple of minutes.

Add the stock to the pan and bring to a gentle simmer. Stir in the oregano, tomato purée and salt cod, cover and cook very gently for about 25 minutes until the cod is very tender.

Stir the spaghetti into the pan and cook for 5 minutes until almost tender. Stir in the tomatoes and cabbage leaves and cook for a further 5 minutes. Season to taste with salt and pepper and serve in bowls.

For homemade fish stock, melt 15 g (½ oz) butter in a large saucepan and gently fry 1 kg (2 lb) white fish bones and trimmings until the trimmings have turned opaque. Add a quartered onion, 2 roughly chopped celery sticks, a handful of parsley, several lemon slices and 1 teaspoon peppercorns. Cover with cold water and bring to a gentle simmer. Cook very gently for 30–35 minutes. Strain through a sieve and leave to cool. Cover and chill for up to 2 days or freeze for up to 3 months.

vegetarian

masala dahl with sweet potato

Serves **4**

Preparation time **15 minutes**

Cooking time **50 minutes**

3 tablespoons **vegetable oil**

2 **onions**, chopped

2 **garlic cloves**, crushed

½ teaspoon **dried chilli flakes**

1.5 cm (¾ inch) piece of **fresh root ginger**, grated

2 teaspoons **garam masala**

½ teaspoon **ground turmeric**

250 g (8 oz) **dried split yellow peas**, rinsed and drained

200 g (7 oz) **can chopped tomatoes**

1 litre (1¾ pints) **vegetable stock** (see page 210 for homemade)

500 g (1 lb) **sweet potatoes**, scrubbed and cut into small chunks

200 g (7 oz) **spinach**, washed and drained

salt

naan breads, to serve

Heat the oil in a saucepan and fry the onions for 5 minutes. Add the garlic, chilli flakes, ginger, garam masala and turmeric and cook, stirring, for 2 minutes.

Add the split peas, tomatoes and 750 ml (1¼ pints) of the stock and bring to the boil. Reduce the heat, cover and cook gently for 20 minutes until the peas have started to soften. Add more stock if the mixture runs dry.

Stir in the sweet potatoes, re-cover and cook for a further 20 minutes until the potatoes and peas are tender, adding more stock if necessary to keep the dahl juicy. Tip the spinach into the pan and stir until wilted. Add a little salt to taste. Serve with warmed naan breads (see below for homemade) and mango chutney.

For homemade spiced naan breads, to serve as an accompaniment, mix together 250 g (8 oz) strong white flour, 1 teaspoon crushed coriander seeds, 1 teaspoon crushed cumin seeds,1 teaspoon salt and 1 teaspoon easy-blend dried yeast in a bowl. Add 2 tablespoons natural yogurt and 125 ml (4 fl oz) warm milk and mix with a round-bladed knife to a soft dough, adding a dash more water if it feels dry. Knead on a lightly floured surface for 10 minutes (or use a freestanding mixer with dough hook attachment, kneading for 5 minutes). Turn into a bowl, cover with clingfilm and leave to rise for about 1 hour until it has doubled in size. Turn out on to a floured surface and divide into 4 equal pieces. Roll out each into a tear shape about 22 cm (8½ inches) long. Heat a griddle or dry frying pan until hot and cook the breads for 2–3 minutes on each side until puffed and lightly browned.

all-in-one veggie breakfast

Serves **4**
Preparation time **10 minutes**
Cooking time **35 minutes**

500 g (1 lb) **cooked
    potatoes**, cubed
4 tablespoons **olive oil**
few **thyme sprigs**
250 g (8 oz) **button
    mushrooms**, trimmed
12 **cherry tomatoes**
4 **eggs**
2 tablespoons chopped
    parsley, for scattering
salt and **pepper**

Spread the potato cubes out in an even layer in a roasting tin. Drizzle over 2 tablespoons of the oil, scatter over the thyme sprigs and season with salt and pepper. Bake in a preheated oven, 220°C (425°F), Gas Mark 7, for 10 minutes.

Stir the potato cubes well, then add the mushrooms and return the roasting tin to the oven for a further 10 minutes. Add the tomatoes and return the tin to the oven for a further 10 minutes.

Make 4 hollows in between the vegetables and carefully break an egg into each hollow. Return the tin to the oven for a final 3–4 minutes until the eggs are set.

Scatter the parsley over the top and serve straight from the tin.

For all-in-one veggie supper, without the eggs, cook the recipe above using 750 g (1½ lb) potatoes and 400 g (13 oz) mushrooms. Then sprinkle 125 g (4 oz) grated Cheddar cheese over the vegetables for the final 10 minutes of cooking.

pappardelle with pea shoots & dill

Serves **2**
Preparation time **5 minutes**
Cooking time about
   12 minutes

200 g (7 oz) **dried**
   papperdelle or other ribbon
   pasta
50 g (2 oz) **butter**
1 **garlic clove**, crushed
2 tablespoons chopped **dill**
50 g (2 oz) **Parmesan**
   cheese, freshly grated
50 g (2 oz) **pea shoots**, thick
   stalks discarded
lemon wedges, for squeezing
   over
salt and **pepper**

Bring a large saucepan of salted water to the boil.
Add the pasta and cook for 8–10 minutes or until just
tender. Drain and return to the pan.

Dot the butter on to the hot pasta and add the garlic,
dill, Parmesan and a little salt and pepper. Stir until well
mixed, then add the pea shoots and stir until slightly
wilted and distributed through the pasta.

Serve immediately with lemon wedges for squeezing
over the pasta.

For spaghetti carbonara with olives & basil, beat
together 1 whole egg, 2 egg yolks, 100 ml (3½ fl oz)
single cream, 40 g (1½ oz) freshly grated Parmesan
cheese, 1 crushed garlic clove and a little salt and
pepper in a bowl. Cook 200 g (7 oz) dried spaghetti
or linguini in a large saucepan of lightly salted boiling
water for 8 minutes or until tender. Drain and return to
the pan. Add the egg mixture and 50 g (2 oz) chopped
pitted black olives. Stir until the eggs are lightly cooked
in the heat of the pasta, returning to the heat very briefly
if necessary. Serve immediately, scattered with plenty of
torn basil leaves.

pesto & lemon soup

Serves **6**
Preparation time **10 minutes**
Cooking time **25 minutes**

1 tablespoon **olive oil**
1 **onion**, finely chopped
2 **garlic cloves**, finely chopped
2 **tomatoes**, skinned (see
    page 11) and chopped
1.2 litres (2 pints) **vegetable
    stock** (see page 210
    for homemade)
1 tablespoons **ready-made
    pesto**, plus extra to serve
grated rind and juice of
    1 **lemon**
100 g (3½ oz) **broccoli**, cut
    into small florets, stems sliced
150 g (5 oz) **courgettes**,
    diced
100 g (3½ oz) **frozen podded
    soya beans**
65 g (2½ oz) **small dried
    pasta shapes**
50 g (2 oz) **spinach**, washed,
    drained and shredded
salt and **pepper**
basil leaves, to garnish
    (optional)
sun-dried tomato focaccia or
    ciabatta, to serve

Heat the oil in a saucepan and gently fry the onion for 5 minutes until softened. Add the garlic, tomatoes, stock, pesto, lemon rind and a little salt and pepper and simmer gently for 10 minutes.

Add the broccoli, courgettes, soya beans and pasta shapes and simmer for 6 minutes.

Stir the spinach and lemon juice into the pan and cook for 2 minutes until the spinach has just wilted and the pasta is just tender.

Ladle the soup into bowls, top with extra spoonfuls of pesto and garnish with a few basil leaves, if liked. Serve with warmed olive or sun-dried tomato focaccia or ciabatta bread.

For homemade Parmesan thins, to serve as an alternative accompaniment to the bread, line a baking sheet with nonstick baking parchment and sprinkle 100 g (3½ oz) freshly grated Parmesan cheese into 18 well-spaced mounds on to the lined baking sheet. Bake in a preheated oven, 190°C (375°F), Gas Mark 5, for 5 minutes or until the cheese has melted and is just beginning to brown. Leave to cool and harden, then peel off the lining paper and serve the thins on the side with the soup.

pepper stew & cheese toasties

Serves **4**
Preparation time **25 minutes**
Cooking time **50 minutes**

6 tablespoons **olive oil**
800 g (1 lb 9 oz) **mixed red,
    green** and **orange peppers**,
    cored, deseeded and cubed
1 **onion**, thinly sliced
1 large **fennel bulb**, trimmed
    and thinly sliced
3 **garlic cloves**, crushed
2 x 400 g (13 oz) **cans
    chopped tomatoes**
300 ml (½ pint) **vegetable
    stock** (see page 210)
1 tablespoon **light
    muscovado sugar**
4 tablespoons **sun-dried
    tomato paste**
2 teaspoons **ground paprika**
2 teaspoons **fennel seeds**,
    lightly crushed
salt

Toasties
2 **panini breads**
2 tablespoons **olive oil**
2 teaspoons **capers in brine**
100 g (3½ oz) **goats' cheese**
2 tablespoons chopped
    lovage or **basil**

Heat the oil in a large heavy-based frying pan and gently fry the peppers, onion and fennel slices, stirring frequently, for 20–25 minutes until the vegetables are soft and pale golden.

Stir in the garlic, tomatoes, stock, sugar, tomato paste, paprika and fennel seeds and bring to the boil. Reduce the heat, cover with a lid or foil and simmer gently for a further 20 minutes until the stew is thick and pulpy. Season to taste with a little salt.

Slice the panini breads in half and drizzle the cut sides with the oil. Rinse and drain the capers. Slice the goats' cheese and use with the capers and lovage or basil to sandwich the breads together. Heat a large dry frying pan or ridged griddle pan until hot and cook for 2–3 minutes on each side until golden, pressing the breads down with a fish slice to flatten. Cut into chunky pieces and serve with the pepper stew.

For cheese & lovage dumplings, to serve as an alternative accompaniment to the toasties, mix together 200 g (7 oz) self-raising flour, 100 g (3½ oz) vegetable suet, 75 g (3 oz) grated mature Cheddar cheese and 2 tablespoons chopped lovage in a bowl. Add a little salt and pepper and 150 ml (¼ pint) cold water and mix with a round-bladed knife to a soft dough. Divide the mixture into 8 pieces and shape each roughly into a ball. Add to the cooked stew and cover with a lid or tented foil to trap the steam. Cook for 20 minutes until the dumplings are light and fluffy.

warm greek salad

Serves **4**
Preparation time **10 minutes**
Cooking time **25 minutes**

8 **ripe tomatoes**, roughly
  chopped
2 **green peppers**, cored,
  deseeded and roughly
  chopped
1 small **red onion**, thinly sliced
2 **garlic cloves**, crushed
2 tablespoons chopped
  oregano
6 tablespoons **extra virgin
  olive oil**
200 g (7 oz) **feta cheese**
12 **pitted black olives**
salt and **pepper**
pitta breads, to serve

Scatter the tomatoes, green peppers and onion in a shallow ovenproof dish.

Mix the garlic with the oregano, oil, plenty of pepper and a little salt. Drizzle the mixture over the vegetables. Bake in a preheated oven, 200°C (400°F), Gas Mark 6, for 10 minutes.

Crumble the feta into small pieces and scatter over the vegetables along with the olives. Return the dish to the oven for a further 15 minutes. Serve warm with toasted pitta breads.

For garlic bread sauce, to serve as an accompaniment, tear a small pitta bread into pieces and place in a bowl with 5 tablespoons milk. Leave to stand for 5 minutes until the bread has softened. Lift the bread out of the bowl and squeeze out the excess milk. Place the bread in a food processor and add 2 crushed garlic cloves and 50 ml (2 fl oz) olive oil. Process to a smooth paste. Add a further 50 ml (2 fl oz) oil and 2 tablespoons white wine vinegar and process again to a paste. Season to taste with salt and pepper and transfer to a serving bowl. Cover and chill until ready to serve.

green bean & potato pot

Serves **4**
Preparation time **25 minutes**
Cooking time **50 minutes**

350 g (11½ oz) **runner beans**, topped and tailed, then cut into thin slices
200 g (7 oz) **French beans**, topped and tailed, then halved
150 g (5 oz) **podded baby broad beans**
2 tablespoons **olive oil**
1 large **onion**, finely chopped
700 g (1 lb 6 oz) **potatoes**, cut into small chunks
4 **garlic cloves**, crushed
2 tablespoons **sherry vinegar**
2 tablespoons **grainy mustard**
2 tablespoons **light muscovado sugar**
2 **bay leaves**
400 g (13 oz) **can chopped tomatoes**
3 tablespoons **sun-dried tomato paste**
salt and **pepper**

Bring a large saucepan of water to the boil. Add the runner and French beans and cook for 5 minutes. Add the broad beans and cook for a further 1 minute. Drain and set aside. Wipe out the pan.

Heat the oil in the pan and gently fry the onion and potatoes, turning frequently, for 5 minutes. Cover and cook very gently for a further 10 minutes or until the potatoes are softened and beginning to colour.

Stir in the garlic, vinegar, mustard, sugar, bay leaves, tomatoes and tomato paste. Bring to the boil, then reduce and gently simmer, uncovered and stirring frequently, for 15 minutes until the sauce is very thick.

Add all the beans to the pan and stir well. Heat through gently for 10 minutes, adding a dash of water to the pan if the mixture runs dry. Season to taste with salt and pepper before serving.

For Catalonian ratatouille, to serve with the green bean and potato pot, heat 2 tablespoons olive oil in a large saucepan or frying pan and gently fry 1 large diced aubergine for 5 minutes. Add 3 cored, deseeded and diced red peppers, 1 chopped onion and a further 2 tablespoons oil. Cook gently, stirring, for 5 minutes. Add 2 crushed garlic cloves, 5 skinned and chopped tomatoes and a little salt and pepper. Cover and cook gently for 10 minutes. Stir well and cook, uncovered, for a further few minutes if necessary until the stew is thick and pulpy. Serve with warmed bread.

fig, goats' cheese & tapenade tart

Serves **4**
Preparation time **10 minutes**
Cooking time **20–25 minutes**

350 g (11½ oz) **ready-made puff pastry**, defrosted if frozen
plain flour, for dusting
beaten egg, to glaze
3 tablespoons ready-made or homeade **olive tapenade** (see page 122)
3 **ripe figs**, quartered
100 g (3½ oz) **cherry tomatoes**, halved
100 g (3½ oz) **soft goats' cheese**, crumbled
2 teaspoons chopped **thyme**
2 tablespoons freshly grated **Parmesan cheese**

Roll out the pastry on a lightly floured surface until 2.5 mm (1/8 inch) thick into a rectangle 20 x 30 cm (8 x 12 inches), trimming the edges.

Prick the pastry with a fork and score a border 2.5 cm (1 inch) in from the edges. Transfer to a baking sheet. Brush the pastry with beaten egg to glaze and bake in a preheated oven, 200°C (400°F), Gas Mark 6, for 12–15 minutes.

Remove the pastry from the oven and carefully press down the centre to flatten slightly. Spread the centre with the tapenade and then arrange the figs, tomatoes, goats' cheese, thyme and Parmesan over the top.

Return the tart to the oven for a further 5–10 minutes until the pastry is golden, the cheese has melted and the figs are cooked. Brown the top under a preheated hot grill, if liked, making sure that the pastry edges don't burn (you can cover them with foil). Serve warm with a rocket salad, if liked.

For grilled vegetable & goats' cheese tart, thinly slice 1 courgette and 1 aubergine, core, deseed and quarter 1 red pepper and cut 1 red onion into thin wedges. Brush the vegetables with olive oil and cook under a preheated hot grill for 3–4 minutes on each side until tender. Cook the recipe above using the grilled vegetables instead of the figs and tomatoes.

blackened tofu with fried rice

Serves **2**
Preparation time **25 minutes**,
  plus marinating
Cooking time **20 minutes**

1 **hot green chilli**, deseeded
  and roughly chopped
50 g (2 oz) **fresh root ginger**,
  peeled and roughly chopped
2 **garlic cloves**, roughly
  chopped
2 tablespoons **dark
  muscovado** or **molasses
  sugar**
3 tablespoons **soy sauce**
200 g (7 oz) **firm tofu**
3 tablespoons **vegetable oil**
  or **wok** or **stir-fry oil**
1 bunch of **spring onions**,
  chopped
175 g (6 oz) **baby corn**, cut
  diagonally into 1 cm (½ inch)
  slices
150 g (5 oz) **Chinese
  cabbage**, shredded
275 g (9 oz) **pack cooked
  white long-grain rice** or
  frozen rice
5 tablespoons chopped **fresh
  coriander**

Blend the chilli, ginger, garlic, sugar and 2 tablespoons soy sauce in a small food processor to a loose paste. Drain the tofu and pat dry on kitchen paper. Cut into chunks. Mix with the chilli paste in a non-metallic bowl, then cover and leave to marinate for 1–2 hours.

Heat 1 tablespoon of the oil in a frying pan or shallow flameproof casserole over a high heat. When very hot, tip in the tofu mixture and fry quickly, turning occasionally, for 5 minutes, until browned on all sides. Lift out with a slotted spoon on to a plate.

Add the remaining oil to the pan, stir in the spring onions and corn and stir-fry for 3–4 minutes until beginning to brown. Add the cabbage and stir-fry for 2 minutes. Tip in the rice and coriander and stir-fry for a further 5 minutes until the rice is thoroughly hot. Drizzle with the remaining soy sauce, stir in the coriander and scatter with the tofu. Cook for a further 1 minute.

For herb & lentil pilaf, heat 3 tablespoons vegetable oil in a frying pan or shallow flameproof casserole and gently fry 1 chopped onion and 2 chopped celery sticks until softened. Add 1 teaspoon crushed cumin seeds, 1 cinnamon stick and 1 teaspoon mild chilli powder. Cook, stirring, for 2 minutes. Stir in 750 ml (1¼ pints) vegetable stock and bring to the boil. Add 200 g (7 oz) rinsed and drained dried green lentils and cook gently for 5 minutes. Add 200 g (7 oz) uncooked white long-grain rice and cook for a further 12–15 minutes until both rice and lentils are tender, adding a little more stock if the mixture runs dry. Drizzle with the juice of 1 lime and stir in 6 tablespoons chopped parsley and 4 tablespoons chopped fresh coriander before serving.

okra & coconut stew

Serves **3–4**
Preparation time **15 minutes**
Cooking time **40 minutes**

375 g (12 oz) **okra**
4 tablespoons **vegetable oil**
2 **onions**, chopped
2 **green peppers**, cored,
    deseeded and cut into
    chunks
3 **celery sticks**, thinly sliced
3 **garlic cloves**, crushed
4 teaspoons **Cajun spice**
    blend
½ teaspoon **ground turmeric**
300 ml (½ pint) **vegetable
    stock** (see page 210 for
    homemade)
400 ml (14 fl oz) **can coconut
    milk**
200 g (7 oz) **frozen
    sweetcorn**
juice of **1 lime**
4 tablespoons chopped **fresh
    coriander**
salt and **pepper**

Trim the stalk ends from the okra and cut the pods into
1.5 cm (¾ inch) lengths.

Heat 2 tablespoons of the oil in a large deep-sided
frying pan or shallow flameproof casserole and fry the
okra for 5 minutes. Lift out with a slotted spoon on
to a plate.

Add the remaining oil to the pan and very gently fry
the onions, peppers and celery, stirring frequently, for
10 minutes until softened but not browned. Add the
garlic, spice blend and turmeric and cook for 1 minute.

Pour in the stock and coconut milk and bring to the boil.
Reduce the heat, cover and cook gently for 10 minutes.
Return the okra to the pan with the sweetcorn, lime
juice and coriander and cook for a further 10 minutes.
Season to taste with salt and pepper and serve.

For easy cornbread, to serve as an accompaniment,
mix together 150 g (5 oz) cornmeal, 100 g (3½ oz)
plain flour, 1 teaspoon salt, 2 teaspoons baking powder,
½ teaspoon ground cumin and ½ teaspoon dried chilli
flakes in a bowl. Beat 1 egg with 200 ml (7 fl oz) milk
and add to the bowl. Mix gently until just combined (do
not overmix). Turn into a greased 600 ml (1 pint) loaf tin.
Bake in a preheated oven, 190°C (375°F), Gas Mark
5, for 30 minutes until firm to the touch. Serve warm or
transfer to a wire rack to cool.

sicilian caponata

Serves **4**
Preparation time **15 minutes**,
  plus standing
Cooking time **30 minutes**

100 ml (3½ fl oz) **olive oil**
2 **aubergines**, cut into 3.5 cm
  (1½ inch) cubes
1 large **onion**, coarsely
  chopped
3 **celery sticks**, sliced
50 g (2 oz) **pine nuts**
2 **garlic cloves**, chopped
400 g (13 oz) **can plum
  tomatoes**, drained and
  roughly chopped
2 tablespoons **capers in
  brine**, rinsed and drained
50 g (2 oz) **pitted green
  olives**
3 tablespoons **red wine
  vinegar**
1 tablespoon **caster sugar**
6 **basil leaves**
salt and **pepper**
crusty bread, to serve

Heat the oil in a large frying pan over a high heat until the oil begins to shimmer and fry the aubergines in two batches, stirring frequently, for 5–6 minutes until golden and tender, lifting out with a slotted spoon into a bowl.

Pour off all but 2 tablespoons of the oil from the pan. Add the onion, celery and pine nuts and gently fry for 10 minutes until the vegetables are softened and lightly golden. Return the aubergines to the pan and stir in all the remaining ingredients except the basil. Season to taste with salt and pepper.

Bring to the boil, then reduce the heat and simmer for 5 minutes. Stir in the basil. Remove from the heat and leave to stand for at least 15 minutes to allow the flavours to mingle.

Serve warm or cold, as an antipasto, side dish or a vegetarian main course, with some crusty bread on the side.

For potato & pepper caponata, peel and cut 500 g (1 lb) potatoes into 3.5 cm (1½ inch) cubes. Cook in a saucepan of salted boiling water until tender, then drain. Heat 4 tablespoons olive oil in a.frying pan and gently fry the onion, celery and pine nuts as above, along with 2 red peppers, cored, deseeded and cut into large chunks. Toss in the potatoes and the remaining ingredients as above, using 50 g (2 oz) black olives instead of the green olives. Season to taste with salt and pepper and finish cooking as above.

asparagus & new potato tortilla

Serves **4**
Preparation time **15 minutes**
Cooking time **40 minutes**

350 g (11½ oz) **asparagus spears**
400 g (13 oz) **new potatoes**
100 ml (3½ fl oz) **olive oil**
1 **onion**, chopped
6 **eggs**
5 g (¼ oz) **basil leaves**, torn into pieces
salt and **pepper**

Snap off the woody ends of the asparagus and cut the spears into 5 cm (2 inch) lengths. Slice the potatoes very thinly.

Heat 50 ml (2 fl oz) of the oil in a sturdy frying pan about 25 cm (10 inch) across. Add the asparagus and fry gently for 5 minutes until slightly softened. Lift out with a slotted spoon on to a plate. Add the remaining oil to the pan and scatter in the potatoes and onion. Cook very gently, turning frequently in the oil, for about 15 minutes until the potatoes are tender.

Beat the eggs with a little salt and pepper in a bowl and stir in the basil leaves. Add the asparagus to the pan and combine the vegetables so that they are fairly evenly distributed. Pour the egg mixture over the vegetables and reduce the heat to its lowest setting. Cover with a lid or foil and cook for about 10 minutes until almost set but still a little wobbly in the centre.

Loosen the edge of the tortilla, cover the pan with a plate and invert the tortilla on to it. Slide back into the pan and return to the heat for 2–3 minutes until the base has firmed up. Slide on to a clean plate and serve warm or cold, cut into wedges.

For hollandaise sauce, to spoon over the tortilla, put 1 tablespoon white wine vinegar in a food processor with 2 egg yolks. Blend lightly to combine. Cut 150 g (5 oz) butter into pieces and melt gently in a small saucepan. Pour into a jug. With the machine running, very slowly pour in the melted butter until thick and smooth. Season to taste with salt and pepper and add a dash of hot water if the sauce is very thick.

spiced chickpeas with kale

Serves **4**
Preparation time **10 minutes**
Cooking time **35 minutes**

3 tablespoons **vegetable oil**
3 **red onions**, cut into wedges
2 tablespoons **mild curry paste**
400 g (13 oz) **can chopped tomatoes**
400 g (13 oz) **can chickpeas**, drained
300 ml (½ pint) **vegetable stock** (see page 210 for homemade)
2 teaspoons **soft light brown sugar**
100 g (3½ oz) **curly kale**
salt and **pepper**

Heat the oil in a large saucepan and fry the onions for 5 minutes until beginning to colour. Stir in the curry paste and then the tomatoes, chickpeas, stock and sugar.

Bring to the boil, then reduce the heat, cover and simmer gently for 20 minutes.

Stir in the kale and cook gently for a further 10 minutes. Season to taste with salt and pepper and serve.

For sesame flatbreads, to serve as an accompaniment, place 250 g (8 oz) plain flour, 1 teaspoon salt and 25 g (1 oz) sesame seeds in a bowl. Add 3 tablespoons vegetable oil and 125 ml (4 fl oz) cold water and mix with a round-bladed knife to a dough, adding a dash more water if the dough feels dry. Divide into 8 pieces and very thinly roll out each piece on a lightly floured surface until about 2.5 mm (1/8 inch) thick. Heat a griddle or large dry frying pan until hot and cook the flatbreads for about 2 minutes on each side until pale golden. Serve warm.

squash, kale & mixed bean soup

Serves **6**
Preparation time **15 minutes**
Cooking time **45 minutes**

1 tablespoon **olive oil**
1 **onion**, finely chopped
2 **garlic cloves**, finely chopped
1 teaspoon **smoked paprika**
500 g (1 lb) **butternut squash**, peeled, deseeded and diced
2 small **carrots**, diced
500 g (1 lb) **tomatoes**, skinned (optional – see page 11) and roughly chopped
410 g (13½ oz) **can mixed beans**, drained
900 ml (1½ pints) **vegetable stock** (see page 210 for homemade)
150 ml (¼ pint) **crème fraîche**
100 g (3½ oz) **kale**, torn into bite-sized pieces
salt and **pepper**
focaccia, to serve

Heat the oil in a saucepan and gently fry the onion for 5 minutes until it is softened. Stir in the garlic and smoked paprika and cook briefly, stirring, then add the squash, carrots, tomatoes and beans.

Pour the stock into the pan, season to taste with salt and pepper and bring to the boil, stirring. Cover and simmer for 25 minutes or until the vegetables are tender.

Stir the crème fraîche into the soup, then add the kale, pressing it just beneath the surface of the stock. Re-cover and cook for 5 minutes until the kale has just wilted.

Ladle into bowls and serve with warm focaccia.

For cheesy squash, pepper & mixed bean soup, fry the onion in the oil, then add the garlic, smoked paprika, squash, tomatoes and beans as above, adding a cored, deseeded and diced red pepper instead of the carrots. Pour in the stock, then add 65 g (2½ oz) Parmesan rinds and season to taste with salt and pepper. Cover and simmer for 25 minutes. Stir in the crème fraîche as above but omit the kale. Discard the Parmesan rinds, ladle the soup into bowls and top with freshly grated Parmesan to serve.

artichoke & barley risotto

Serves **4**
Preparation time **25 minutes**
Cooking time **45 minutes**

400 g (13 oz) **Jerusalem artichokes**
50 g (2 oz) **butter**
300 g (10 oz) **pearl barley**
150 ml (¼ pint) **dry white wine**
500 ml (17 fl oz) **hot vegetable stock** (see below for homemade)
125 g (4 oz) **mascarpone cheese**
50 g (2 oz) **mixed herbs**, such as chives, parsley, tarragon and dill
finely grated rind of 2 **lemons**
freshly grated **Parmesan cheese**, for sprinkling
salt and **pepper**

Scrub and thinly slice the artichokes. Melt the butter in a large saucepan and very gently fry the artichokes, stirring, for 10 minutes until beginning to soften.

Add the pearl barley and cook, stirring, for 2 minutes. Stir in the wine and cook quickly for 2–3 minutes until the wine has been absorbed. Gradually add the hot stock to the pan, a ladleful at a time, and cook, stirring frequently, until each ladleful has been absorbed. Continue to cook, adding a ladleful of stock at a time and stirring frequently until each ladleful has mostly been absorbed before adding the next. This should take about 20–25 minutes, by which time the barley should be tender but retaining a little bite. Add a little more stock if needed.

Stir the mascarpone, herbs and lemon rind into the risotto and cook for a further 2 minutes. Season to taste with salt and pepper and serve sprinkled with grated Parmesan.

For homemade vegetable stock, heat 1 tablespoon vegetable oil in a large saucepan and gently fry 2 washed, unpeeled and roughly chopped onions, 2 roughly chopped carrots, 2 each roughly chopped celery sticks, parsnips and courgettes and 200 g (7 oz) trimmed and sliced mushrooms, stirring frequently, for 10 minutes until softened. Add 3 bay leaves and a handful of parsley and thyme sprigs. Cover with 1.5 litres (2½ pints) cold water and bring to the boil. Reduce the heat and simmer very gently, uncovered, for 40 minutes. Strain through a sieve and leave to cool. Cover and store in the refrigerator for up to several days or freeze for up to 6 months.

carrot, lentil & tahini soup

Serves **4**
Preparation time **10 minutes**
Cooking time **45 minutes**

2 tablespoons **sesame seeds**,
plus extra for sprinkling
2 tablespoons **olive oil**
1 **onion**, chopped
500 g (1 lb) **carrots**, chopped
1 litre (1¾ pints) **vegetable
stock** (see page 210 for
homemade)
2 teaspoons chopped **lemon
thyme leaves**, plus extra for
sprinkling
150 g (5 oz) **dried green
lentils**, rinsed and drained
5 tablespoons **tahini paste**
crème fraîche or **Greek
yogurt**, for topping
salt and **pepper**

Heat the sesame seeds in a large dry saucepan until
lightly toasted. Tip out into a small bowl.

Add the oil to the pan and gently fry the onion and
carrots for 10 minutes until softened. Add the stock and
thyme and bring to the boil. Reduce the heat, cover and
cook very gently for 10 minutes.

Tip in the lentils, cover and cook gently for a further
20 minutes or until the lentils are soft. Remove from the
heat, leave to stand for 5 minutes and then and stir in
the tahini paste. Season to taste with salt and pepper.

Ladle into bowls and top with spoonfuls of crème
fraîche or Greek yogurt. Serve sprinkled with extra
sesame seeds and thyme.

For garlic-fried pitta breads, to serve as an
accompaniment, slice 4 regular pitta breads horizontally
through the centres to make 8 thin slices. Whisk
together 4 tablespoons olive oil, 1 crushed garlic clove,
½ teaspoon crushed fennel seeds and a little salt and
pepper in a small bowl. Brush over both sides of the
pitta breads. Heat a griddle or large dry frying pan until
hot and cook the breads for a couple of minutes on
each side until pale golden and crisp. Serve warm with
the soup.

provençal vegetable stew

Serves **4**
Preparation time **15 minutes**
Cooking time **55 minutes**

4 tablespoons **olive oil**, plus
   extra for drizzling
1 large **red onion**, sliced
4 **garlic cloves**, chopped
2 teaspoons **ground
   coriander**
1 tablespoon chopped **thyme**
1 **fennel bulb**, trimmed and
   sliced
1 **red pepper**, cored,
   deseeded and sliced
500 g (1 lb) **vine-ripened
   tomatoes**, diced
300 ml (½ pint) **vegetable
   stock** (see page 210 for
   homemade)
125 g (4 oz) **Niçoise olives**
2 tablespoons chopped
   parsley
slices of **crusty bread**,
   to serve
salt and **pepper**

Heat the oil in a large saucepan and gently fry the onion, garlic, coriander and thyme, stirring frequently, for 5 minutes until the onion is softened. Add the fennel and red pepper and cook, stirring frequently, for 10 minutes until softened.

Stir in the tomatoes and stock and season to taste with salt and pepper. Bring to the boil, then reduce the heat, cover and simmer gently for 30 minutes.

Add the olives and parsley to the pan and simmer, uncovered, for a further 10 minutes.

Meanwhile, heat a ridged griddle pan until hot and cook the bread slices until toasted and lightly charred on both sides. Drizzle liberally with oil.

Serve the stew hot with the toasted bread slices.

For pasta with Provençal sauce, cook the stew as above. Towards the end of the cooking time, cook 450 g (14½ oz) dried penne in a large saucepan of lightly salted boiling water for 10–12 minutes until just tender. Drain well and serve the pasta topped with the vegetable stew as a pasta sauce, sprinkled with freshly grated Parmesan cheese and scattered with basil leaves.

parsnip, sage & chestnut soup

Serves **4**
Preparation time **15 minutes**
Cooking time **50 minutes**

3 tablespoons ready-made
    or homemade **chilli oil** (see
    below for homemade), plus
    extra for drizzling
40 **sage leaves**
1 **leek**, trimmed, cleaned and
    chopped
500 g (1 lb) **parsnips**, roughly
    chopped
1.2 litres (2 pints) **vegetable
    stock** (see page 210 for
    homemade)
pinch of **ground cloves**
200 g (7 oz) **pack cooked
    peeled chestnuts**
2 tablespoons **lemon juice**
crème fraîche, for topping
salt and **pepper**

Heat the chilli oil in a large saucepan until a sage
leaf sizzles and crisps in 15–20 seconds and fry the
remaining leaves in batches until crisp, lifting out with
a slotted spoon on to a plate lined with kitchen paper.
Set aside.

Add the leek and parsnips to the pan and fry gently for
10 minutes until softened. Add the stock and cloves and
bring to the boil. Reduce the heat, cover and cook very
gently for 30 minutes until the vegetables are very soft.
Stir in the chestnuts and cook for a further 5 minutes.

Blend the soup using an immersion blender or in a
food processor. Add the lemon juice and reheat gently,
seasoning to taste with salt and pepper.

Ladle into bowls, top with a little crème fraîche and
drizzle sparingly with extra chilli oil. Serve scattered with
the sage leaves.

For homemade chilli oil, pour 300 ml (½ pint) olive
oil into a saucepan. Add 6 whole dried chillies, 2 bay
leaves and 1 rosemary sprig and heat through gently
for 3 minutes. Remove from the heat and leave to cool
completely. Using a jug or funnel, pour into a thoroughly
clean glass jar with a clip top or cork seal, adding the
chillies and herbs. Cover and store in a cool place for
a week before using. The oil will become hotter during
storage. Use as above, or in pasta and pizza recipes or
any dishes where you want to add a little heat.

barley, beer & mushroom cobbler

Serves **4**
Preparation time **30 minutes**
Cooking time about **1¾ hours**

50 g (2 oz) **butter**
500 g (1 lb) **cup mushrooms**,
  trimmed and thickly sliced
1 large **onion**, sliced
1 small **swede**, diced, about
  450 g (14½ oz), peeled
  and diced
1 tablespoon **plain flour**
400 ml (14 fl oz) **strong ale**
300 ml (½ pint) **vegetable
  stock** (see page 210 for
  homemade)
75 g (3 oz) **pearl barley**
2 tablespoons **grainy mustard**
1 tablespoon chopped
  rosemary
4 tablespoons **single cream**

Cobbler
175 g (6 oz) **self-raising flour**,
  plus extra for dusting
100 g (3½ oz) **slightly salted
  butter**, cut into small pieces
75 g (3 oz) **Gruyère cheese**,
  grated
50 ml (2 fl oz) **milk**, plus extra
  to glaze

Melt half the butter in a flameproof casserole and fry the mushrooms for 10 minutes. Lift out and set aside. Melt the remaining butter in the casserole and fry the onion and swede for 8–10 minutes until beginning to colour. Add the flour and cook, stirring, for 1 minute. Blend in the ale, then the stock. Bring to the boil and add the pearl barley, mustard and rosemary. Cover and cook in a preheated oven, 180°C (350°F), Gas Mark 4, for 50 minutes to1 hour until the barley is tender.

Make the cobbler. Place the flour in a food processor, add the butter and process until the mixture resembles breadcrumbs. Add the Gruyère and milk and process to a thick dough, adding a dash more milk if dry. Tip out on to a floured surface and roll out to 1.5 cm (¾ inch) thick. Cut out rounds using a 4 cm (1¾ inch) cutter, re-rolling the trimmings. Increase the oven temperature to 220°C (425°F), Gas Mark 7. Stir the mushrooms and cream into the casserole and check the seasoning. Arrange the scones around the edge and brush with milk. Return to the oven, uncovered, for 20–25 minutes until golden.

For cauliflower & celeriac cobbler, melt 25 g (1 oz) butter in a flameproof casserole and fry 1 large sliced onion until softened. Add 1 large cauliflower, cut into florets, 450 g (14½ oz) peeled and diced celeriac, 2 teaspoons crushed cumin seeds, ½ teaspoon celery salt and ¼ teaspoon cayenne pepper. Fry gently for 5 minutes. Add 2 tablespoons flour and cook, stirring, for 1 minute. Remove from the heat and blend in 750 ml (1¼ pints) vegetable stock. Bring to the boil, cover and cook as above, adding the cream and finishing with the scone topping. Sprinkle with chopped parsley and serve.

spiced black beans & cabbage

Serves **2**
Preparation time **15 minutes**
Cooking time **30 minutes**

40 g (1 ½ oz) **butter**
1 large **onion**, chopped
150 g (5 oz) **baby carrots**, scrubbed
1 tablespoon ready-made or homemade **ras el hanout** spice blend (see below for homemade)
500 ml (17 fl oz) **vegetable stock** (see page 210 for homemade)
200 g (7 oz) **new potatoes**, scrubbed and diced
400 g (13 oz) **can black beans**, rinsed and drained
175 g (6 oz) **cabbage** or **spring greens**
salt (optional)

Melt the butter in a saucepan and gently fry the onion and carrots for 5 minutes until the onion is softened. Add the spice blend and fry for 1 minute.

Pour in the stock and bring to the boil. Reduce the heat to its lowest setting and stir in the potatoes and beans. Cover and cook gently for 15 minutes until the vegetables are tender and the juices slightly thickened.

Cut away the thick stalks from the cabbage and discard, then roll up the leaves and finely shred. Add to the pan and cook for a further 5 minutes. Season with salt, if necessary, and serve.

For homemade ras el hanout spice blend, place ½ teaspoon each cumin, coriander and fennel seeds in a mortar and crush with a pestle. Add 1 teaspoon yellow mustard seeds and ¼ teaspoon each ground cinnamon and cloves and grind the spices together. Alternatively, use a small coffee or spice grinder to grind the spices.

vegetable & mascarpone bake

Serve **4**
Preparation time **15 minutes**
Cooking time **1¾ hours**

75 g (3 oz) **butter**
500 g (1 lb) **fennel bulbs**
1 tablespoon **lemon juice**
450 g (14½ oz) **courgettes**, sliced
250 g (8 oz) **mascarpone cheese**
4 **eggs**
2 **garlic cloves**, crushed
100 g (3½ oz) **Emmental cheese**, grated
150 ml (¼ pint) **milk**
2 tablespoons chopped **parsley**
salt and **pepper**

Dot the butter into a shallow 2 litre (3½ pint) ovenproof dish and place in a preheated oven, 180°C (350°F), Gas Mark 4, for 5 minutes until melted. Meanwhile, roughly chop the fennel, reserving the fronds. Toss the fennel in the melted butter, drizzle with the lemon juice and season with salt and pepper. Mix well. Cover and bake for 40 minutes.

Add the courgettes and stir the ingredients together. Return to the oven, uncovered, for a further 30 minutes. Beat the mascarpone with the eggs, garlic, half the Emmental and the milk. Pour over the baked vegetables and sprinkle with the remaining Emmental. Reduce the oven temperature to 150°C (300°F), Gas Mark 2, and return the dish to the oven for a further 30 minutes.

Serve with the reserved fennel fronds and parsley.

For summer vegetable & herb frittata, peel an 800 g (1 lb 9 oz) marrow, then halve and scoop out the seeds. Slice the flesh and toss in a bowl with 25 g (1 oz) sea salt. Leave to stand for 20 minutes. Wash the marrow in several changes of cold water to remove the salt and pat dry between layers of kitchen paper. Melt 50 g (2 oz) butter in a frying pan and gently fry the marrow, stirring frequently, for 10 minutes until pale golden. Stir in 2 teaspoons chopped savoury and plenty of pepper. Beat 6 eggs with 4 tablespoons single cream in a bowl and pour into the pan. Heat gently, pushing the mixture from the side of the pan into the centre so that the uncooked eggs fill the space. Once the mixture starts to set, cook gently for a few minutes, then transfer to a preheated moderate grill and cook for about 5 minutes until the surface is golden and the filling is lightly set.

kashmiri pumpkin curry

Serves **4**
Preparation time **20 minutes**
Cooking time **25 minutes**

2 **onions**, quartered
2 **garlic cloves**, peeled
4 cm (1½ inch) piece of **fresh root ginger**, peeled and sliced
1 large **red chilli**, halved and deseeded
1 teaspoon **cumin seeds**, roughly crushed
1 teaspoon **coriander seeds**, roughly crushed
5 **cardamom pods**, crushed
1.4 kg (2¾ lb) **pumpkin**, peeled and deseeded
15 g (½ oz) **butter**
2 tablespoons **sunflower oil**
1 teaspoon **ground turmeric**
1 teaspoon **paprika**
1 **cinnamon stick**, halved
450 ml (¾ pint) **vegetable stock** (see page 210)
150 ml (¼ pint) **double cream**
50 g (2 oz) **pistachio nuts**, roughly chopped
1 small bunch of **fresh coriander**, torn
salt and **pepper**
ready cooked rice and **naan breads**, to serve

Place the onions, garlic, ginger and chilli in a food processor and process until finely chopped, or finely chop by hand. Mix with the crushed cumin, coriander and cardamom.

Slice the pumpkin into 2.5 cm (1 inch) wedges, then cut the wedges in half. Melt the butter with the oil in a large frying pan and fry the pumpkin for 5 minutes until lightly browned. Push the pumpkin to one side of the pan, add the onion mixture and fry for about 5 minutes, until beginning to colour.

Add the turmeric, paprika and cinnamon to the pan and cook briefly, then stir in the stock. Season to taste with salt and pepper and bring to the boil. Reduce the heat, cover and simmer for 10 minutes or until the pumpkin is just cooked.

Stir in half the cream, half the pistachios and half the coriander leaves and gently heat through. Drizzle with the remaining cream and sprinkle with the remaining pistachios and coriander, then serve with ready-cooked rice and naan breads.

For Kashmiri aubergine curry, make the curry as above using 2 large aubergines, cut into 3.5 cm (1½ inch) cubes, in place of the pumpkin and adding 200 g (7 oz) French beans, topped and tailed, then halved, with the stock. Finish as above with the cream and coriander but using 50 g (2 oz) roughly chopped blanched almonds instead of the pistachios.

beetroot & goats' cheese crumble

Serves **4**
Preparation time **25 minutes**
Cooking time **1½ hours**

1 kg (2 lb) **beetroot**
500 g (1 lb) **small onions**,
  quartered
4 tablespoons **olive oil**
½ teaspoon **caraway seeds**
75 g (3 oz) **plain flour**
1 tablespoon chopped **lemon
  thyme**, plus extra to garnish
40 g (1½ oz) **butter**, cut into
  small pieces
200 g (7 oz) **soft goats'
  cheese**, thinly sliced
salt and **pepper**

Scrub the beetroot and cut into thin wedges. Place in a shallow ovenproof dish with the onions and drizzle with the oil. Sprinkle with the caraway seeds and season with a little salt and plenty of pepper. Cook in a preheated oven, 200°C (400°F), Gas Mark 6, for about 1 hour until the vegetables are roasted and tender, stirring once or twice during cooking.

Meanwhile, place the flour and lemon thyme in a bowl, add the butter and rub in with the fingertips until the mixture resembles fine breadcrumbs.

Scatter the goats' cheese over the vegetables and sprinkle with the crumble mixture. Return to the oven for 25–30 minutes until the topping is pale golden. Sprinkle with thyme and serve with a watercress or rocket salad, if liked.

For roasted roots with horseradish crumble, peel and cut 750 g (1½ lb) parsnips and 500 g (1 lb) celeriac into small pieces and place in a shallow ovenproof dish with 500 g (1 lb) small red onions, quartered. Drizzle with olive oil and cook in the oven as above. Prepare the crumble topping as above. Mix 200 ml (7 fl oz) single cream with 2 tablespoons hot horseradish sauce and pour over the roasted vegetables, then sprinkle over the crumble and bake as above.

goats' cheese & pepper lasagne

Serves **4**
Preparation time **20 minutes**
Cooking time **50 minutes –
1 hour**

325 g (11 oz) **can or jar
pimientos**
6 **tomatoes**, skinned (see
page 11) and roughly
chopped
1 **yellow pepper**, cored,
deseeded and finely
chopped
2 **courgettes**, thinly sliced
75 g (3 oz) **sun-dried
tomatoes**, thinly sliced
100 g (3½ oz) **sun-dried
tomato pesto**
25 g (1 oz) **basil**
4 tablespoons **olive oil**
150 g (5 oz) **soft goats'
cheese**, crumbled
600 ml (1 pint) ready-made or
homemade **cheese sauce**
(see below)
150 g (5 oz) **dried egg
lasagne**
6 tablespoons **grated
Parmesan cheese**
salt and **pepper**
salad leaves, to serve

Drain the pimientos and roughly chop. Place in a bowl
with the tomatoes, yellow pepper, courgettes, sun-dried
tomatoes and pesto. Tear the basil leaves and add to
the bowl with the oil and a little salt and pepper. Mix
together thoroughly.

Cover a quarter of the tomato mixture into a 1.8 litre
(3 pint) shallow ovenproof dish and dot with a quarter
of the goats' cheese and 4 tablespoons of the cheese
sauce. Cover with a third of the lasagne sheets in a
layer, breaking them to fit where necessary. Repeat the
layering, finishing with a layer of the tomato mixture and
goats' cheese.

Spoon with the remaining cheese sauce and sprinkle
with the Parmesan. Bake in a preheated oven, 190°C
(375°F), Gas Mark 5, for 50 minutes–1 hour until deep
golden. Leave to stand for 10 minutes before serving
with a leafy salad.

For homemade cheese sauce, place 500 ml
(17 fl oz) milk in a saucepan with 1 small onion and
1 bay leaf. Heat until just boiling, then remove from
the heat and leave to infuse for 20 minutes. Strain the
milk into a jug. Melt 50 g (2 oz) butter in the cleaned
saucepan, add 50 g (2 oz) plain flour and stir in quickly.
Cook over a medium heat, stirring, for 1–2 minutes, then
remove from the heat and gradually whisk in the infused
milk until blended. Return to the heat, bring gently to the
boil, stirring, and cook for 2 minutes until the sauce has
thickened. Remove from the heat and stir in 125 g
(4 oz) grated Cheddar or Gruyère cheese until melted.

index

234

238

acknowledgements

Commissioning Editor: Eleanor Maxfield
Editor: Jo Wilson
Art Direction and Design: Penny Stock
Designer: Eoghan O'Brien
Stylist: Kim Sullivan
Photographer: William Shaw
Home Economist: Joanna Farrow
Picture Library Manager: Jennifer Veall
Copy-Editor: Jo Richardson
Proofreader: Alison Bolus
Indexer: Diana LeCore
Production Controller: Sarah Kramer

Special Photography: © Octopus Publishing Group Limited/
William Shaw

Other Photography: © Octopus Publishing Group/167; Stephen
Conroy 41, 57, 67, 85, 89, 103, 129, 147, 189, 203; Will Heap 125,
153; David Munns 49, 59; Lis Parsons 27, 229; William Shaw 197,
209, 225; Ian Wallace 16, 18, 79, 95, 109, 135, 185, 215.